Books by Christopher Merrill

Workbook (poems)

Outcroppings: John McPhee in the West (editor)

Fevers & Tides (poems)

The Forgotten Language: Contemporary Poets and Nature (editor)

From the Faraway Nearby: Georgia O'Keeffe as Icon (editor, with Ellen Bradbury)

The Grass of Another Country: A Journey Through the World of Soccer (prose)

Anxious Moments, prose poems by Aleš Debeljak (translator, with the author)

Watch Fire (poems)

WATCH FIRE

WATCH FIRE

Poems by
Christopher Merrill

With an Introduction by
David St. John

White Pine Press

Grateful acknowledgement is made to Teal Press for permission to reprint previously
published poems from *Workbook,* copyright ©1988 by Christopher Merrill; and *Fevers
& Tides,* copyright ©1989 by Christopher Merrill.

Translation acknowledgements:
"Voici," "L'Amour," and "Les Poumons" from *Le Marteau Sans Mâitre* by René Char.
José Corti, 1934.

"Intérieur" from *Poèmes 1940-1943* by André Breton. Editions Gallimard, 1948.

"Horal," "Miss X," and excerpts from "Como pájaros perdidos" from *Nuevo recuento
de poemas* by Jaime Sabines. Editorial Joaquín Mortiz, S.A., 1977.

I am also grateful to the editors of the following publications, in which several poems
from *Luck* first appeared: *Columbia: A Magazine of Poetry & Prose, The Guadalupe
Review, The Journal, Mississippi Review, Pivot, Poetry East, Poetry Wales, Prairie
Schooner, River Styx, The South Florida Poetry Review,* and *The Taos Review.*

I wish to thank Agha Shahid Ali, Phil Foss, Brewster Ghiselin, Elizabeth Grossman,
Robert Jebb, W.S. Merwin, Leslie Norris, Pattiann Rogers, David St. John, and
Frederick Turner for their support and suggestions.

My thanks as well to Jerry Johnston for his help in translating the poetry of Jaime
Sabines.

Lastly, I would like to express my gratitude to the Ingram Merrill Foundation for a
grant which made completion of this book possible.

Publication of this book was made possible, in part,
by grants from the National Endowment for the Arts
and the New York State Council on the Arts.

Book design by Elaine LaMattina

Manufactured in the United State of America

ISBN 1-877727-43-1

First printing, 1994

White Pine Press · 10 Village Square · Fredonia, New York 14063

CONTENTS

IV. The Sea

Fevers & Tides

Luck

I.

II.

III.

IV.

WATCH FIRE

and the firesmoke of mankind everywhere . . .
— St.-John Perse

*For my parents
and for Lisa*

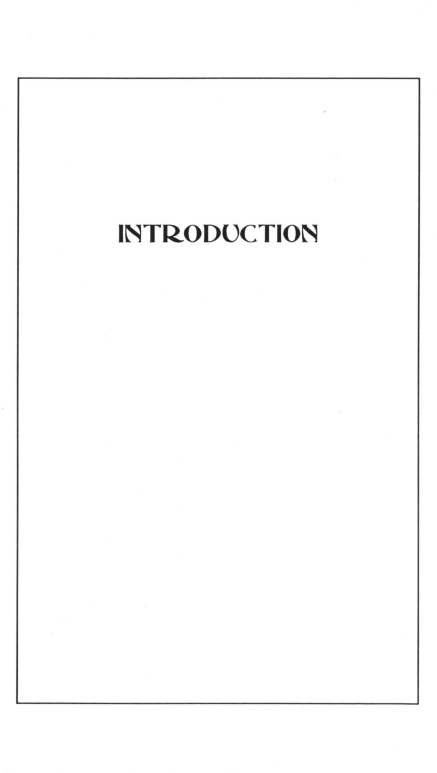

INTRODUCTION

For those of us who have loved Christopher Merrill's poetry for so many years, it is sometimes startling to recall that he is that rarest of creatures on the landscape of contemporary poetry, a "complete" writer. By that I mean he is a writer in the European tradition that assumes, in addition to one's primary genre, a writer necessarily does other kinds of writing as well — journalism, non-fiction essays (often what we now call "personal" essays), reviews, editorial work for journals and/or books, and of course translation.

So let's first acknowledge Christopher Merrill's superb work as an editor: of *Outcroppings: John McPhee in the West;* of the gorgeous book entitled, *From the Faraway Nearby: Georgia O'Keeffe as Icon;* and of the very successful anthology of nature poetry, *The Forgotten Language.* In addition, he is the co-translator of both André Breton's *Constellations* and a wonderful collaborative work by Breton, René Char, and Paul Eluard, *Slow Down Construction.* He has also translated, with the author, a collection of prose poems, *Anxious Moments,* by Aleš Debeljak. Let's not forget too that Christopher Merrill has written the most important book about the world of soccer ever to appear in the United States, a fascinating account of the 1990 World Cup called *The Grass of Another Country.* Lastly, his essays and reviews have appeared in many journals and newspapers. And, recently, he has been spending time in the former Yugoslavia while working on his newest non-fiction work, *Only the Nails Remain: Three Balkan Journeys.*

Yet it is Christopher Merrill's poetry that draws us as readers with this marvelous volume of his collected work. His poetry often posits the natural world as the powerful backdrop of those shifting currents of our own desires and disappointments, fragile memories and disparate hopes. In these poems, the real world is constantly interrupted by the visionary instant, by a revelatory sleight-of-hand we find in the "fevers & tides" of consciousness. Here are works of eloquence and subtlety and, as Galway Kinnell has put it in *The Book of Nightmares,* of great "tenderness toward existence."

Christopher Merrill's first collection, *Workbook,* provides us with a hymnal of childhood and a magical sketchbook of the natural world. These poems are celebratory and incantatory fables of the emerging self, all revealing those elegiac shadows that touch each passage through a life. These lessons of the self unfold in both the peopled and the natural worlds, and the uneasy intersection of those worlds is a concern that runs through all of Merrill's work. Yet the surety and beauty of nature is sometimes troubled by his poems' queries into mankind's problematical place there.

There is a charged, magical air to these poems. Even in Merrill's self-portraits (and their reflections of possible selves: imagined, historical, and actual), or in his "work" songs of the elemental and the daily, it is this magical sense that helps provide the restitution of a belief in our world. These poems touch upon our inability to really connect; instead, we act out our assumed and self-defined (and self-limiting) "roles." For Christopher Merrill, this is the tragedy we fight against always. The concluding poem of *Workbook,* the poem entitled, "The Sea," offers us the consolations of nature – the regenerative, salty human taste of the sea – while exposing that world's lost inhabitants as they collide, miss each other yet again, yet constantly return like the seasons in a fateful season of hope.

I remember when I first read the poems of Christopher Merrill's second collection, *Fevers & Tides;* I was struck by the maturity and absolute authority of the voice in that work. I was thrilled by "Charm," the invocation to a muse, for a muse, coming as it does immediately after the devastating opening poem, "Words." In this book, once again, the overriding presence of the natural world exists as the backdrop against which all of these poems are enacted with their human scenes and dilemmas. Yet these poems remain meditations on the human spirit. With their wonder and wisdom, their modesty and clarity of vision, they recall the work of Merrill's true mentor, that fine poet, Brewster Ghiselin. Still, there is something so individual about these poems; their narrative fragments seem fraught with suggestion, implication, and fabular resonance. These stories flicker and spin like a medallion hung in the moonlight, dangling from the frame of an open window, each glinting turn revealing some new aspect of the poet's meditation.

In *Fevers & Tides,* the question that recurs is: How do we slash through the dense foliage and undergrowth of words? What machete might we use to clear a simple path along our way? Only, the poems say, with a blade forged of faith, love and conscience. I know it sounds corny when I say it; the poems make it eloquent. Merrill knows that the very medium of our human exchange helps, all too frequently, to obfuscate our true ability to make connections with each other. And so we find, in some of his poems, an attention to the more oblique conjunctions of language and phrase we sometimes call surrealism, though for this poet I would suggest it is a kind of hyper-realism rather than any fancy meta-realism.

For Merrill, the special perspective of the fairy tale or fable often seems most accurate to experience, just the right lens with which to reveal his vision of our world. Just as the surrealism of *Workbook* was of the kind of psychological intensity found in, say, the Brothers Grimm, so too this surrealism recalls the line from Merrill's version of a Jaime Sabines poem: "I prefer my old hallucinogens: solitude, love, death." Merrill's is not a classic surrealism of combined disparate elements; it provides a greater imaginative permission for objects and observations to discover their magnetic and gravitational equivalents or resemblances. What could be more natural since, as Stevens said, our world is a world of resemblances?

Throughout his work, Christopher Merrill has invoked both Roethke and Frost, sometimes overtly and sometimes covertly. He returns to the same issues they echo: human desire and human resignation set against the natural order and its cycles of will, defeat, and hope. In the new poems of this collection, those of the volume *Luck,* Merrill once again surprises us by moving into an even broader field of vision and ambition. His amazing poem, "Pike Place Market Variations," stands in the tradition that recently includes Galway Kinnell's "The Avenue Bearing the Initial of Christ into the

New World," and which harkens back to Whitman's finest bardic yawp. Yet there is also a delicate homage to the poets Elizabeth Bishop and Carlos Drummond de Andrade, "The Sirens," as well as a Kafkaesque, somewhat apocalyptic, snowbound and snowblind burlesque of a long poem entitled, "White Noise." It is, as they say, a romp.

But the culmination of all of Christopher Merrill's poetry to date has to be the astonishing poem, "Luck." In this blank verse operetta, we find secret (and bald) allusions veining its lines: Stevens raises his shaggy head once again, and even the good Doctor Williams is given a wry nod. This savagely funny and moving poem reminds us that all luck isn't good — more often, the luck we receive from the Gods of Whatever is bad, bad, bad. Yet the seeming fatedness of our lives and all natural cycles is always tempered by our resilience, by our own fierce impulse to resist the very notion of fate. However comic the situations this leads us into, Merrill suggests that we need to have compassion for our grand noble foolishness. Besides, however random the events of a life, however accidental everything might seem, the poet knows that "accidents, like art,/ Have formal patterns, invisible designs." And it is the revelation of those patterns and designs that Merrill does best; he lets us enjoy those swirling eddies of chance that move our lives from place to place, year to year. Of course, they are the eddies moving also ever closer to the lip of the bottomless falls . . .

I envy the reader who comes to this work for the first time. The riches and surprises will be many. To those of you who are, like me, returning to these poems with the same pleasure of a hiker on beloved terrain, let's all wish ourselves safe footing and some kind of bloody luck.

— David St. John

WATCH FIRE

WORKBOOK

There is a clock that does not strike.
— Arthur Rimbaud

The Guests

Now in the evening, the guests rub the lead
Glass in the window and watch the moon dissolve.
Out back, an old man bends a guitar string
Around the silver light, tuning the air
To the lulling sounds of rain, to the high clouds
That gather there at dusk and disappear
Before the wind rises, and to the flashing
Of fireflies trapped in the heat, in the milk bottles
On the porch, where a sleeping child is dreaming
Of llamas and lutes . . .
                    And if the earth begins
To hum, and the dry wells refill themselves,
The guests may close their eyes—and sing.

I.
LESSONS

Childhood

Newspapers scarred the stream;
Words swirled in the eddies;
Grey figures — a dead thief,
The President and his wife,
Two race horses — floated past
And sank . . .
                Or snagged the rocks
Rippling the slow water
Until the sun, like a man
With a knife, cut them apart
So they could sail away.

. . .

On the last night, outside my tent, someone
Startled the woods: a flashlight fluttered; twigs,
Like small animals, crackled underfoot;
Mosquitoes buzzed the netting. I held my breath
To hear the hushed voices, a muffled cough,
A siren down the road . . .
                A match was struck.
I crawled outside: my mother and my father,
Dressed in white, stood near the sumac, waving
Their hands of fire. They touched the trees, they licked
Their palms, and rose above the burning woods.

Fable

How the gravestones smiled!
And clouds, like flowers,
Settled over the trees
In arrangements of grey,
When I hid on the hill
To watch my funeral.

My mother, in sackcloth
And ashes and at attention
(Minister's orders), wept
Until my father hoisted
My casket up into an opening
In the clouds, where it floated

Among the swirling leaves
And shadows, like a sheath
Of bark launched on a stream —
It was then she laughed,
And cast her flowers overhead,
And danced a jig around my grave . . .

And when he gave my casket
A push, and it sailed to the sun,
And I rolled down the hill
To follow the chosen one,
She joined the crowd in silence,
Tears hardening on her lips.

A Boy Juggling a Soccer Ball

after practice: right foot
to left foot, stepping forward and back,
   to right foot and left foot,
and left foot up to his thigh, holding
   it on his thigh as he twists
around in a circle, until it rolls
   down the inside of his leg,
like a tickle of sweat, now catching
   and tapping on the soft
side of his foot, and juggling
   once, twice, three times,
hopping on one foot like a jump-roper
   in the gym, now trapping
and holding the ball in midair,
   balancing it on the instep
of his weak left foot, stepping forward
   and forward and back, then
lifting it overhead until it hangs there;
   and squaring off his body,
he keeps the ball aloft with a nudge
   of his neck, heading it
from side to side, softer and softer,
   like a dying refrain,
until the ball, slowing, balances
   itself on his hairline,
the hot sun and sweat filling his eyes
   as he jiggles this way
and that, then flicking it up gently,
   hunching his shoulders
and tilting his head back, he traps it
   in the hollow of his neck,
and bending at the waist, sees his shadow,
   his dangling T-shirt, the bent

blades of brown grass in summer heat;
  and relaxing, the ball slipping
down his back . . . and missing his foot.

  He wheels around, he marches
over the ball, as if it were a rock
  he stumbled into, and pressing
his left foot against it, he pushes it
  against the inside of his right
until it pops into the air, is heeled
  over his head — the rainbow! —
and settles on his extended thigh before
  rolling over his knee and down
his shin, so he can juggle it again
  from his left foot to his right foot
— and right foot to left foot to thigh —
  as he wanders, on the last day
of summer, around the empty field.

Concert

When the catalpa's seedpods drop
At dusk and harden into drumsticks,
A child hears, against the curb,
The leaves' brush strokes; and, underfoot,
The chestnuts click like castanets
Until a bell ushers him in.

Soon the wind's curtains rise; and branches,
Like bows, scrape his bedroom window,
Introducing the simple cadences
Of rain, the syncopation of hail,
And the storm's measure to the boy,
Who drums his fingers on the sill,

Keeping time.

Children's Suite

I. Seaglass

Buffed in the ocean's tumbler,
Polished with sea wrack and sand,
Rolled and lulled like dice
Around the North Atlantic,
It bears the voices of sailors,
Of men and women shrieking
In the game rooms and cabins
Of sinking ships, of the sea
Itself, to the deaf child
Collecting shells at low tide.

II. Tongue-Tied

I forgive my tongue's clipped wings,
The rusted scissors, the nod;
The cluttered kitchen table
On which they laid me down;
The smoke in the doctor's eyes;
The bourbon shaking his hand;
My father, who fainted twice;
And my mother, flecked with blood,
Who should have known better; —
For my blood tasted like milk,
A birdcall swelled in my throat,
And my first words let me fly.

III. First Questions

Whose eyes rolled my shadow
Into a little ball? Whose heart
Bounced it to the window?
Whose breath let it fall

To the ground? And whose feet
Dribbled it down the street
Until the child fishing
For snakes in the gutter
Received it from the leaves
And passed it to his father,
Who let it fall to pieces
Before the sun went down?

IV. Correspondences

The stems of seven daffodils
Leaning against the lip of the glass,
Like the pencils, bolts, and nails
That filled the mason jars
Lining my father's workbench,
Unravel near the top and hide
In the bowed heads of the flowers,
Like the cigarettes that grew
Out of his mouth, and nose, and ears
On Sundays, driving home from church.

The Parade: July 4th, 1970

Where the main road disappeared
Around a bend of trees and boulders —
Washed downhill in the last storm — firemen
Carried our village with them: floats,
Horses and guns, a marching band . . .
But the road, like a shallow stream
Boys will tramp across, cleared again.

Then nine young men, dressed in black robes,
Barefoot and hooded in the heat,
Followed their elders through the town,
An empty coffin on their shoulders.
Silenced by the procession, our porches
Crackled once the light-soaked road
Swallowed the chanting men and their coffin.

The Fishing Jacket

for Lyall Merrill 1902-1970

Mothballed in a Salvation Army box,
His khaki jacket reeks of salmon eggs —
When I shake it out, flecks settle in the closet,
Like cinders, and the leaders of black thread
Dangling in the empty buttonholes begin
To shiver. A tuft of feathers brushes past —
Too small for birds, his tied flies hook my fingers.

And on the shelf by the cracked window, an urn —
His ashes: *He was such a little man,*
My grandmother said at the service, passing
The urn to the minister — and everyone laughed . . .

Now I, too, must laugh: his sleeves cover my hands.

. . .

In my war dream, I wear
A field commander's coat.
North Africa. The front,
Where Rommel's scent is faint,

And General Patton's spilled
His bourbon in our tent
Again . . . The desert sun,
That sewing needle, pricks

My skin, stitching my memory
Into the sand. I drift
Around the camp, I unravel
A cigarette and let

The French tobacco fly
In the wind. *Our casualties,*
I tell the good general,
Have been heavy. He smiles.

And when he stares at the name
Splayed above my shirt pocket,
I hold my breath, believing
He can keep a secret.

. . .

I put her out of her pain
Was the first line of my first song.

I sang my six-year-old triumph
At dusk, at the orchard's frayed edge,

Where my cairn — seven bricks — balanced
On top of a red-winged blackbird —

With a broken wing — swayed in the wind,
Where a soft trill caught in her throat.

No, my grandfather muttered, *not
Like that!* And slipped the bricks off one

By one. He cupped the dying bird
In his large yellow shaking hands,

He dusted her wings, he set her in
The bushes. *She will heal herself,*

He said, marching me up the hill.
And I believed him, having returned

Nine times already from the dead
That day, imagining each death

Lasted only until I climbed
A tree to hide from my slow friends . . .

The flies at daybreak — they were pinned
Like medals to my blackbird's wings.

So I gripped the rusted belt
Girding an apple tree, I pulled

Myself up to its cement sealer.
All day, among the ripening

Fruit and migrating birds, I hid
From the sky, which knows my song by heart.

• • •

And when I open the window, two plates of glass
Slide down the ivy and fall into the garden
Without breaking . . .
                    Scatter his ashes and wait,
I tell myself. *Wait.*

Lessons

In the Sunday *Times:* a spread of photographs
From the Lodz ghetto, grainy takes of the end —
I stare and stare at a locksmith: the key
Is his six-pointed star. These are the steps
No one can climb, this the soup line, and this
The *babka* made of ground potato peels —
And here's an advertisement: *Take a good
Long look* . . . A woman in a white silk shirt
(Stamped and numbered on the order form)
Clutches her belt, smiling for the camera.

. . .

What could I learn from you whose bruisings bore
The imprints of shoes and phones? who turned my back
Into a checkered map of dog brush marks?
Who made my wrists and fingers swell, like balloons . . .
Begetters of my silence and my wrath,
I learned from your refrain — *If I have to,
I'll beat the truth out of you!* — to lie, to speak
In signs (*Don't touch!*), to whisper and hide; and then
How hard it is to untie myself from you
When I wind these words around our common wounds.

. . .

The snap and rise and dip of my sidearm
Slider, the whistle of my sucker pitch
Sweeping the spring air clean, the ancient wish
Of my stone whirring across the field — these caught
Him in the eye . . . *Because I did, because
He cheated us again, because I had it
In my hand* — Mr. Chrenko took my hand,
Spat out a Yiddish curse and, twisting my arm
Around the light I'd stolen from his son,
Condemned me to a life of wandering.

II.

NOTES FOR A SELF-PORTRAIT

Sacrilege

These are my credentials: I traveled
To Egypt when I was a younger man
And tunneled into a pyramid.

With a rope tied to a rock
By the entrance, I picked my way
Through the dust and rubble for the better

Part of a week until I found —
In the corner of a false tomb, under
A pile of stones — the passage to the burial room.

Paintings covered the walls:
Harvest time, hunting, the sacrifice
Of animals. Twelve alabaster

Vases surrounded a sarcophagus,
Where the last king slept
His serpentine sleep . . .

I chiseled the ivory and gold
From his wooden furniture, slipped the silver
Jewelry off his arms and legs, smashed

His pottery against the walls. Then
I followed the rope back,
Over the waters, to England . . .

Now when I say I stole my eyes
From the dead, just remember one thing:
I'm the thief you sent for.

Poaching

*"You'd have to be able... to see
what steals I've made and used."*
— Charles Wright

At dusk, in the rusted light of August, I hummed like a wire
Along the fence dividing the widow's land
Into thirds, into the past,
                    present, and future perfect
Tenses of the verb *to have* in its holy trinity
Of greed, and skimmed
                    my voice across the pond, the warm air,
The waves and watery tops of timothy and alfalfa,
To scare her horses imported from Russia
              and the black men poaching in our woods.

. . .

In Fergus Tufts' field, shucking ears of corn
And whistling through the skins: a buck and a doe,
Feeding nearby, looked up and did not scare
Until I slipped away, the stalks stripped clean,
Our dinner tucked underarm, like a newspaper.

And when I climbed the bridle path, holding
The fence to keep from sliding down the muck,
The gully of horseshoes, and broken rails,
And cigarette butts scuffed into hoofprints,
A host of spirits tracked me through the woods,

Singing a song of the grief stitched, like stripes,
Into the fabric of my innocent needs.

. . .

Thus a scattering of seeds plundered from memory's husk —

At noon, through the trees, the way the light's riptide and roll confuse the story line;

A bundle of oil-soaked rags, or the smell of singed flesh;

Names like Clarence Nagro, "Mad" Anthony Wayne, Tempe Wick;

A horse hidden in a bedroom, corn and apples rotting under the floorboards, and soldiers plotting in the snow;

A barn fire, and Tanya's stallions galloping into the sky; —

And then, at dusk, the way the round heads of red clover bob in the wind, marking the far side of silence.

. . .

"If you mean to kill me, shoot me now!"
Cried General Wayne, opening his coat. "Here's
My heart." And his drunken soldiers reeled away
With fixed bayonets, fifes and drums, the cannon,
And one hundred head of cattle from the compound —
His Pennsylvania Line, knee-deep in snow,
Veering barefoot between Vealtown and Princeton.

New Year's night, 1781 —
Talbot and Bettin dead; Henry Wick's daughter
Stopped on the road, then followed home (her horse,
To the men's astonishment, "just disappeared");
And now, an unpaid month of building and
Rebuilding huts and redoubts ending in
Revolt, a volley fired — overhead — at him . . .

Still, he chose to ride with those who'd lived

On dogs, birch bark, roasted shoes. "Their business was
With Congress" — not with him. They'd worshipped him,
Like sons, this band of laborers and bounty-
Seekers; and, like the helpless father who
Must watch his children make their own mistakes,
He headed for Princeton and imprisonment . . .

. . .

For memory invents its own network of new connections —

At daybreak, from the footbridge, I watched Tanya's friend lead a
white horse down to the stream, and shoot it.

All afternoon the stench of rotting flesh staining the air, the swamp
grass, the stones.

". . . Because Clarence is illiterate," my father explained, explaining
nothing.

But when the rank water filled our pond, the clouds' boats sailed
past without signaling, stranding me there.

And when the barn burned down that fall, I saw a fleet of slave
ships blazing in a distant harbor.

— Then I heard the beginning and the end of speech and song.

. . .

But here invention flags before the facts:
When Sam Tufts (volunteer fire chief, Babe Ruth
Team coach, and plumber) choked a black-robed boy
One Fourth of July, honoring the war
In Asia and the memory of his nephew —
Fergus' son — by protesting the students'

Protest of our parade (their coffin lay
In pieces near the judges' stand), the sun
Burned through the fittings in the clouds and burst
Into the students' song . . . Soon a horse van came
To spirit them away, and the firemen raised
Their hands. My first pitch rattled the batting cage.

. . .

Smoke drifted overhead. The woods blazed
With signs: scars on a stranger's face. And when the last thread
Of light broke in the sky, and a gust of wind
Swept the smoke away, I knelt in the blackberry brambles
And wept. I licked my wrists. Tasted juice. Blood. Then footsteps,
Voices whispering beyond the fence, and my heart,
Like a fist, opening in the dark,
To lead me home again.

The Diver

was balanced on the edge of the platform
when a word appeared like a moon, gathered in clouds,
and swirled above his hands and eyes — he jumped
upwards and out, tucking his legs and head
into his body's shell and, somersaulting
backwards, searching the ceiling for a polestar,
he cracked his skull on the platform, nicking
the dormant seed of his own death, and dropped
feet first, head slumped, slicing through the air,
the water, bleeding from his mouth and ears,
to root himself on the bottom of the pool
and see the springboards fluttering in their sheaths,
the whole crowd on their feet, speaking in tongues,
a woman waving a broken fist or a flower,
then a light rising through the crimson water:
the sun the sailor takes his warning from.

The Gatekeeper

after Kafka

Awake again at the twisted iron gate,
Where the Chinese girl is still on guard. To enter
The city, in which I hope to find the lost
Messenger, I must sign my name on her
Black silk skirt. But my names, my various
Signatures, never seem to work. Thus I offer
New ones: Savonarola, Gabriel
Fahrenheit, William Cody — she smiles, but no.

To keep her attention (she's easily distracted),
I tell her about the blind pianist
Who hammered his black keys together, nailing
His hymn to my door, like an old wreath, I even
Hum a few bars. She leans against the gate,
Wincing. As usual, the glittering mosques
In the distance prompt me to repeat my story
About the freighters lighting up the harbor:

How they change into candles at midnight;
How they burn their iron wicks, turning the water
To wax; and how, as the bridge begins to melt,
The cars dissolve into the vanishing road; —
She sighs, as if to say, *It's come to this?*
There I am! I cry. *On a mountaintop. Fasting.*
While General Sherman marches to the sea.
She raises an eyebrow, considering.

His armies leave a trail of smoke behind,
I continue, my confidence mounting, *and the tears*
Of women after rape. The defeated soldiers
Stand apart, heads down, shoeless and drunk . . .

But when I notice her smiling again,
I lose my place, I start to falter: *Horses*
With burning eyes are neighing in the night –
She frowns. So I hurry on, ignoring her:

I hear a steady drumbeat in the wind.
I've been there now a week, and nothing's changed.
Nothing will ever change – she walks away.
Wait! I plead. She stops just long enough
For me to remind her about the sacred
Fish rotting in the artist's studio;
The hourglass opening its mouth to let
The sand return to the sea; the desperadoes

In the Badlands, who held up my westbound coach
And left me in the road, like a rattlesnake
Coiled on a riverbank; – and then she's gone . . .
Once again, I drop to my knees, and on
The scrap of silk she always leaves behind
I paint exactly what I see – the red
Sun surrounded by its twelve silver knives –
Then wait for the horses, the wild horses, to come.

The Knot

A piece of string tied around a tree.
The tree's knotted with disease. A man
Unties the string and holds it in his hands.
As it grows heavy, he lies down.
He drapes it over his chest, spreading
His arms wide. Clouds cover the sun, then pass,
And his lips, his closed eyes, hold the new light.

Beliefs

When the foghorn slashed through the morning, the mist
Bled into the sea, and the wind, baring
Its fists again, bruised the shoreline and the wharves.
The freighters held their breath, like businessmen,
And, skirting the point, disappeared, leaving
Unguents of oil to salve the mangled piers.

. . .

What's important? Stones, beliefs, the blue
Eyes of the woman on the beach, who rode
Her horse to the Dead Sea, who kissed you – once . . .
Say she wore a leather coat, or changed
The color of the clouds, or said she loved you –
What's important is the way she left . . .

. . .

Banish the sea – and the wind, like a frightened child,
Will hug the wavering shore until the sea
Returns . . . And if you ruin the wind, horses
Will canter through the mud, blinding their riders . . .
But cut the horses' throats – and the old words
Will lose their riders, the wind, and the sea again.

The Rope

At the end of the tunnel, where the red light hums, saltwater twists me into the sand.

I smell your ancient perfume in the hair of the walls.

I watch your hands open and close a large oak door; and when I open that door, I discover a rope hanging from a bridge a mile overhead.

I climb the rope, hoisting myself up hand over hand, swinging around in a circle, until you lean over the railing and smile — then cut the rope!

Just before I hit the water, the river freezes over and my body, as it cracks the ice, crumbles into a dream of myself . . .

The door slams shut. The light shatters, the melting ice evaporates.

Crying, clinging to the wall, I crawl out of the tunnel . . . only to find you again, walking up a city street.

Your eyes, when you turn away, burn black — before you disappear, leaving on the sidewalk a trail of charcoal.

A trail I follow out of the city and into the hills, into the forest, where a plume of smoke singes my tongue, granting me the power of speech.

And there you are, in a clearing — surrounded by candles!

I reach for you, begging for light and water.

I know my life will end like this.

Notes for a Self-Portrait

1. Seven finger-splints lined up on my desk, like shotgun shells.
2. Harvesting teeth from the tilled field of my divisions
   and departures.
3. My loose tongue slipping out of its clothes again.
4. A frayed rope of words looped over an ivy-covered wall.
5. A gold piece and a wish – and then another wish.
6. Two stones drying on the windowsill . . . Or: the oxen
   yoked together by a pair of spectacles.
7. The scar sinking into my brow, like dirt settling in a grave.
8. The tangled roots of the cedar toppled in the windstorm
   yielding to the practice of the aspen healing over its
   initialed wounds.
9. Ears that hear bells cracking in the square and the small
   explosions of the clock.
10. Then a charred voice rising out of the ashes of
    another life, another world, whispering *Now begin.*

III.

WORK SONGS

Work Songs

for my father

I. Clearing

The hill in front of our house
Was a maze of brambles, sumac,
And twisted roots, which hid
The road, the trees, and the hill,
Like the tangle of bad dreams —
Forgotten at first light —
That quietly numbs us,
Until my father cleared it
And stood alone on top.

II. Cider-Making

The rasp of gears grinding
In the creaking press, the mash
Of apples clogging the cheesecloth,
The swash and swill of juice
Sluicing down the spillway
Into the wooden tub.

Sticky-fingered, I stacked
The glass jugs filled with juice
In the rusted wheelbarrow,
Then waited for my father — I
Grew cold waiting for my father,
Who grew cold waiting for me.

III. Root-Pruning

He worked all day, digging
A ditch around the apple tree,

Slashing roots with his shovel,
Building a dirt wall around himself.

Dusk falling like rain, like leaves
In hard rain, I filled that ditch
With leaves, fine bark, topsoil,
Banking mulch against the cut roots —

As once, in the dark, he tucked
My blanket up to my chin,
Then turned away — to start new
Roots, stronger roots for winter.

IV. Transplanting

Those blackberry vines arcing
Across the path in the woods,
Tip-rooting in the grass —

When I hacked at the stalks,
Gathering roots to reset in pots,
The wind lashed the canes

To my back; and when I picked
The rotting fruit, a globe
Exploded in my hands, seeding

These words in the air and the earth.

In Spring

for a child

The trees hum in the wind.
And when the wind dies, birds
Fill the trees with song.
In the garden, pea stakes
And sagging onions, stunned
By the hail and hard rain,
Lean in the same direction –
But look: the mustard's sprouted!

From year to year, we learn
What will root, what won't;
Why some birds grow silent
Before the sky clouds over;
And, once, words failing,
Why the grass whispered again.

Epithalamium

for Kitty and Leslie Norris

Bearing the oil-soaked roots
Of a rose, a pair of shears, and a bandanna,
The gardener teeters
On top of the rotting fence, he slides
Along the slippery planks
Like a mountaineer hugging the steep,
Lurches forward and back
And, on the moss-covered corner post, stops.

He sways in the wind,
Trimming the crest of the hemlock hedge,
And laces the garden
To the street, and the street to the sun,
And the sun to the moon
Ribboned with ashes rising from the volcano,
In time for the wedding
Of the maidenhair to the mountaintop.

Housesitting Poems

I. Cowbells

The calf's affected anthem; brass medallion
Of the wind; toll and sign of the sleepwalker; –
These necklaces of bells (bought at an auction),
Hanging from the handles of the double doors,
May wake the blind before they reach the stairs.

II. Carnival

Look: no hands! cries the stripped clock as it ticks
(See the boy standing on the Ferris wheel,
Singing to the crowd gathered by the fence?
The one eyed barker shakes his fist, believing
His son's afraid to jump) and tocks.

III. Findings

A locked trunk. Spoiled meat. Window boxes lined
With mums and sleeping cats. Sunflowers sprouting
Under the bird feeder. Earrings embedded
In the lawn. A peach tree slumped by the garden, yanking
Its curtains down. This urge to look inside.

Workbook

What became of the child
Whose stitches didn't hold,
   Who planted leaves in books?

. . .

Watch the trees slip out of their leaves! It makes them nervous.

They put their ruby leaves in a jewelry box at the wood's edge.

Their yellow skirts drop to the floor.

. . .

When the widow pressed the white keys, the wrinkles in her face
unfolded. She closed her eyes with a smile: her music drifted about
the living room, brushed against the grandfather clock in the corner,
and moved on. Then she shifted her weight on the piano bench and
winced. Her hips, her gnarled fingers ached. She opened her eyes,
grimacing, grinding her teeth. She played on.

. . .

Outside the window,
   Hidden in a patch of poison
      Sumac, books

Are burning –
   The blind man,
      Breathing the itching

Smoke, calls the vines
   Cascading down his trees
      Dangling participles.

. . .

Vines bending the buckeye tree —
Two boys climbing a rope swing.

. . .

Her song measured its steps across the room, charging the warm
air: the curtains yellowed by her husband's cigarette smoke wrapped
her chords in a shroud of ocher light before releasing them; the radi-
ator hissed and spat; a pie tin filled with water and balanced on the
iron gills burbled. Then, unaccountably, she stopped playing . . .

. . .

Why did she leave?
   I remember the grass withering,
   Seeds shriveling in the field, the chirr
   Of locusts heralding the fall,
   What I squandered of my birthright,
   Our covenant with the barbed wire . . .

. . .

Why did she leave?
   I don't remember anymore.

. . .

(The following spring, we spent a morning working in the rain, cut-
ting up the good wood and hauling the weed trees to the pile of
brush, rotten oak beams, and gasoline cans. And when the sun came
out after lunch, we rested on the leaves and branches spread across
the matted earth.
   — What are you thinking about? said my friend.
   An old woman, an upright piano, and three white roses.)

65

. . .

Starting again, I wanted to clear
Everything: the weeds, the raspberry stalks
Ruined by root rot, the sumac vines choking
The buckeye . . .
                   But the stiff vines knotted up —
And, tugging free, I tumbled over backwards
And felt the cool mud seeping through my clothes,
And the warm sun, and my body giving way.

. . .

— What are you thinking about? said my friend.
The girl who laced my hands together with her hair.

. . .

Waking at the sound
Of footsteps, I discover my books
    Fanned out on the floor.

Dusk: three bells,
And the widow sipping rum
    Until her hands stand still.

The plum tree's lost its feathers
— Whoever walks these slick white stairs
    May take wing and fly!

Prayer

Here in the land of salt and stone,

Where the smell of rotting algae and brine shrimp washes over me,
rinsing my eyes and nostrils like the cold;

Where scrub oaks bleed in the hills before the bandages of snow
unravel down the slopes, and the last bees drift with the leaves

Into the canyon streams to shine with the stars;

And where locusts chirr in the saints' blood, and sea gulls fill the
holy square, and steeples lift their hats of smoke and haze to greet
the blind men singing in the street; —

I hear the clock's muffled drums beating again,

And so I repeat my prayer:

I believe in the wind lisping its hallowed song through the keyhole;
in the sound of the latch turning when my desk billows open;

And in the words, as the rug laps against the wall, that guide me
through the channel of the blank page

Out into the open sea.

IV.

THE SEA

Nocturne

No one sees the woman kneeling by the bed of crocuses at dusk.
But she fingers the petals — the white sheets — nervously, wait-
ing for the street to empty.
After the last bus sputters past, she takes off her clothes and hides
them under a juniper.
She climbs into her flower to sleep.
She slips into her yellow nightgown, straightens the collar fringed
with orange, and smiles.
When she pulls the sheets up to her chin, they become sails — they
gather the wind whipping across the Sound.
The song of the flute in the house next door lulls her to sleep, even
as her ketch, this flower, sails across the night sky.
In the morning, in the harbor, the sun beats down on the water, and
her sheets unfold as if by themselves.
She opens one eye.
Mist rises from the grassy leaves surrounding her, dissolving in
the wind.
She stretches her arms above her head.
The first bus stops at the light down the street.
A blind man by the juniper listens for the roar of the bus.
She climbs out of her flower, leaving her nightgown behind, and
vanishes before the bus arrives.

One evening, a man comes to this flower bed and sees a quilt of
violet, yellow, and white folding in on itself.
And when the sun sinks behind the last house on the street, he
kneels in front of one white crocus.
And he touches its petals when no one's looking.
Soon he falls asleep on the wet grass.
And he sleeps through the night.
And then he wakes at dawn as on his first morning at sea —
the wind in his eyes as he walked the slippery deck;
the salt on his tongue, like the taste of his first kiss;
the sun burning his lips when he found himself alone.

The Dancer

She flies to Reno once a month
To see the full moon. Under the sky-
Light in the hotel lobby, she waits,
Empty-handed and alone.

But when the moon appears, and she
Kisses the doorman, and her eyes
Turn into lemons while her clothes
Drop to the floor, the old men cry,

Eighter from Decatur!
Little Phoebe's here again!
Bells ring, lights flash, thousands
Of coins spill out of her mouth.

Stuffing her purple underwear
In his coat pocket, the doorman
Slips out the door and hails a cab
To drive him to the desert.

Seven old women leave their own
Slot machines and, scooping the coins
Up off the floor, reinsert them
In her body, through her seven slots.

She dances around them, pointing
At the moon, smiling. Blackjack tables
Empty. Roulette wheels, like tires, roll
Down the stairs. Crap shooters load

Their guns and hide behind the bar.
Stunned into silence by her dance,
The people sway in the moonlight

Until the manager arrives.

Then the old men cry, *Captain Hicks!*
Captain Hicks! And the old women
Clap their hands. And the crap shooters
Fire at the windows and chandeliers.

The manager clicks his heels.
He knows her whole routine by heart.
He calls her husband, et cetera.
And she takes the next flight home.

The River

Once the storm died down, flocks of blossoms gathered
By the mud-clogged river, the crowd inside
Me knelt in prayer, and I watched you march away.
Soon the clouds returned their verdict, and the crowd
Regained its sense of place, its overweening
Pride, and the river disappeared . . .
                                    Now I wile
My tongue-tied nights away, considering
My leavings: molehills, chickweed, a glass bowl
Of white feathers – my charts of the wind's remains.

Autumn in San Francisco

So late in the fall!
A woman hangs her sheets outside,
And gulls pucker the bay.

Eucalyptus leaves
Stuff the gutters above us —
Are you listening?

More wine! More wine!
The hiss of rain in the fireplace,
The record that we scratched.

Fog horns wake us at dawn —
Mist shrouds the Golden Gate Bridge;
A grey ship slips past.

The sweet scent of your hair
In the afternoon sun, and a blind
Dog brushing the railing.

The mallards on the pond
By the Palace of Fine Arts
Will never leave.

Morning Song

for Lisa

When the wind in the water garden
Rises, like the woman who climbs the chiseled steps
Expecting nothing, hummingbirds flutter down the ledge
To usher in the light of the indolent sun,
Lotus shift their weight, as if to stay
Awake, and the white lilies open
The eyes of the dead, until she lifts her hand
To test the wind . . . Then a sparrow
Squeaks, the water hums, and the reeds pipe and sway.

Love Songs

I. A Covenant

Smoke curls around a tree
Like rope. An old man sighs.
Then a woman ties the rope
To a branch, and they swing
With the ashes in the wind!
Leaves, like watches winding
Down, spill out of their pockets,
Feeding the fire that will carry
Them to the top of the tree,
Curling around them like a rope.

II. Nocturne

When the luna moth (clinging
To the ceiling; to the arc
Of the porch light, like a ring
Of clouds around the moon;
To the memory of the moon,
Which is the song of the woman
Upstairs, naked and alone)
Flutters its wings, the sky
Trembles above the mountains,
And the woman starts to sing.

III. The Dance

Now the empty music stand,
Like a mannequin awaiting clothes,
Pins, and the dressmaker's hand,
Needs the bars and staves of song,
The tablature of joy and grief,
And quick hands, sure hands,

To build — each night — the cell
In which the lovers dance,
Dance until it's time to flee
Down the long white sheets of sleep.

IV. Moonward

In the bathhouse, asleep
By the leaking shower, the lover
Dreaming of the moon: when it drops
Its necklace through the skylight,
The molting rug slithers off;
When it throws its shirt
Over the chair, the windows
Shiver; and when it cuts the rope
Anchoring the house to the earth,
The lover drifts away . . .

V. Aubade

She turns away, as a lily
Stretches for light, her arm dangling
Off the bed, her long fingers
Curling into a fist, and reaches
— In sleep — for the window . . .
Yet he remembers how
They lashed their worn bodies
Together by a tree, building a raft
To float down the river
Flowing through them to the sea.

By the Sea

Beyond the warning sign
Swaying in the loose sand;
Beyond the guardrail that hugs
The bluff, the slick stairway
Down to the sea; and beyond
The sunken/sinking wall
Of weathered logs, of felled
Cedars and spruces that slipped
The clutter of the mill
And drifted through the Sound,
Breaking water until waves
Herded them into shore,
Where workers hauled them off
To build this barricade;
— Beyond all this, the lovers
Huddle in the wind, tending
The clumps of beach grass
Clinging to the last swatch
Of land, to the eroding
Cliff that moves beneath them,
Shifting its weight
Quietly, like a woman
In a rocking chair —
In the house by the sea —
Nursing her child at dawn.

The Sea

The leaves scuttled across the roof,
Because it was autumn; because our house
Lay in the deep shade of maple and oak;
And because I chose the word *scuttled,* thinking
Of the rats who scampered through the cages
And corridors of dream last night, and of waking
At daybreak — alone . . .
                    And because you left,
The leaves scuttle across the roof,
The empty house whispers, *Fall, fall,*
And I smell salt air — and the sea.

FEVERS & TIDES

Tongue, tickle, ethics.
— Julio Cortázar

Words

Paint blistering on the ceiling of the den:
Excuses gathered speed, helping no one.
So I walked up the same mountain as before.

Passed the same barbed wire, broken glass, tire tracks.
Then vetch, and penstemon, and the rusted water
Pipe coursing down through stands of scrub oak, aspen.

In the dry creek: a rattlesnake, coiling,
Guarding the rocks and ripped oak roots, head swaying,
Shaking its only bead, like a fanatic.

I know the little ones can kill: their venom's
Pure as the fury of the lovers' first
Attempts at cruelty, before they learn

What words or gestures will end an argument
Without destroying everything again –
And yet I stood there for a while, listening

To a woodpecker addling an aspen,
A mule deer thrashing in the underbrush,
And near the city thunder rumbling . . .

Some rattlesnakes can grow as long as humans.
This one I sidestepped in the end, then headed
Up the steep part of the trail, holding my tongue.

Charm

A milk snake rustles up the dust and slumber
Of our friends' barn, where I've found room to work,
Or rest, in a stiff-backed chair, with a Shaker table
For a desk, an oil lamp, books; and in the heat
That keeps a watch of swallows on the rafters
I lift my feet, as if to make the wish
A child will make in the back seat of a car
Coasting under a railroad overpass,
The wish to never lose his friends, his parents . . .

And see it slither past a locked trunk, stacks
Of tires, the miniature table and chairs
Collected at an auction for the children
Still in the planning stage, gliding through patches
Of dirt, bird droppings, scuff marks, sweeping the floor
Clean as it slips under my desk, as it hugs
The wall like a thief, as it disappears
Into a hole between the apple bin
And the abandoned stove, and drags itself

Around the closed-off stall, searching the rotting
Floorboards and composted straw for mice, not milk.
The swallows fall like leaves, they whirl around
The barn, they flutter out the door. Above
My desk a wasp rattles the windowpane,
Scaling the glass, then sliding toward the sill.
I hear an airplane stalling in the distance.
By now I'm trembling with my wish, my prayer
To find the words with which to charm you, love.

Catches

*The way things work
is that eventually
something catches.*
                        — Jorie Graham

It's lock step and stab again. The white flag
Raised and aimed at the wall. The body's cold war. —
These clogged knees, these bad drains
And sponges avid for the spirit's wastes,
Click, click . . . If pain's a jagged line drawn from *Here*
To *Here,* a floodlit plain, a fusillade of moments
Exploding underfoot, it is also a prelude
To ritual, to suffusions of grace
Notes brushing their wings over the melody line
In memory's score, and to the appearance of the star
That leaves its tracks everywhere . . . Remember
That bearings can grind their teeth, mustering a crowd
Into action; why edges blur at daybreak,
Disappear at noon, and hone their blades at dusk;
How children buckle their straps, then latch the doors
Behind them; how walls give way; how we plan our next campaigns.

Country Inn

The reformed arsonist hunched over the fire
Escape, guarding himself, whittling a walking stick
Out of a staff of green ash — he's an enigma
To the chambermaid cleaning his room. She finds
On his desk an agate, a polished ashtray, his signature
Scrawled on the blotter. No matches,
Flint, or lighter. Yet she keeps smelling smoke.
She wonders where the owner is, and why
He hasn't called . . . Outside, morning
Glories pinned to the fence, soaking up wood ticks and soot.
Leaves dripping from the honey locust by the road.
Dog days. And the taste of thunder: iron filings. Rain
In a holding pattern, stalling overhead. The airways
Clogged with pollen . . . Emptying
The wastebasket, she sees him, the arsonist,
Pacing the yard, fanning himself, his fingers blazing
A trail she doesn't want to follow, or lose.

Discounts

The innkeeper with his favorite chambermaid, hanging
The flag from the balcony, hasn't forgotten
About his guests — the firemen and the veterans
Marching into town, clutching their coupons, their Independence
Day discounts, like raffle tickets. Yet here are stars
Polished like doorknobs, stripes stiff as collars.
And here's the plunging neckline of Elsie, the Norwegian,
Who works until noon . . . The innkeeper hates
Holidays, and special interest groups, and the way
The daisies in his garden are collapsing, like old boots.
Worse, in number 7, the single vacancy, the ghost of the night
Clerk, the drunk who kicked in the back door
Last New Year's Day, then died at the desk, is acting up
Again. He raps his knuckles on the mirror,
Rattles the glasses stuffed with tissue paper, and stumbles
Into bed . . . The innkeeper would like to believe
He runs a clean joint. That the ghost
Belongs to his imagination. That Elsie doesn't realize
Her blouse is still unbuttoned. That's why he's so careful
With the flag. While his guests weave in the distance, he twists
A red stripe around his finger, proud as the homesteader
Leaning on a fence post at the edge of his range,
Who studied the storm clouds building over the mountains,
Listening for thunder, hoofbeats, the war cries of the Nez Perce.

The Mormon Globes

a display in the library
at the University of Utah

Vision for the westering flocks was contraband,
Like coffee or doubt — yet when the boundaries
Of the Promised Land shifted, despite the prophet's
Word, this pair of globes encased in glass,
This bespectacled illusion, like a sugar baron
In his dotage (with one eye on the New World
And one on Heaven), was smuggled across the sea,
Lugged overland by covered wagon, and lost
Repeatedly, like hope, then faith, and then belief.

The focal point's the way they've aged: the smudged
Names of the rivers and the states, the chipped
And sullied constellations, the blank spaces
And question marks — Nevadas? Galaxies?
What poet wouldn't want to reinvent
The language and the world? And who could foresee
These weapons blooming in the desert, these sheep
Grazing another *poisonous meadow,* these lovers
Rubbing their eyes again, then pointing at the sky?

for Ken Verdoia

In Bountiful

Flushed from its nest, the pygmy owl's a fist of coos
Opening at nightfall; the wind's stalled in the spruces,
Not the afterlife; the new street's breeding lights and limits; —

And I wait, one finger in the air, with the clouds licked
And sealed on the horizon, to be delivered elsewhere.

Cotillions

The ex-greenskeeper in his coat and tails
Plowed up the practice green one night, churning
The spiked and fertilized sod into a punch.
He twisted miniature flags, like swizzle sticks,
Shredded the plastic cups, then seeded the green
In timothy and clover, a mad farmer
Saving a field spent senselessly, like a coin
Lost in a jukebox, in the local diner
Where the couples steeped in gin are drinking coffee,
Arranging a foursome for Saturday.

. . .

A padlocked clubhouse, and stumps of porticoes
Sinking in cement, like palmprints. Quack grass
Raving through the addled and abandoned lawn,
Spreading its message underground: *Listen*
To me, you fools, to me! . . . Against the wall,
Ivy drops its handkerchiefs, and spindle
Trees unspool scarlet yarn, which will wind its way
Around these vacant grounds, soaking up the names
Of the pianist and singer, the chaperones
And guests, the waiters at the last cotillion.

. . .

This tennis court with its nets down, this sea
Of crushed shells lapping against the rusted fence,
This *en tous cas,* is not a poem stripped
Of its music and its meaning; for here are women
In bare feet and long skirts dancing with men
In dungarees, adrift in the green clay
Sparkling with salt, avoiding the white tapes
Nailed into place, like strings of floats, the service
And base lines, the alleys where their children are
Asleep, working the moon for all its light.

90

Ebb Tide

Four o'clock: slogged from silt to seaweed-ribboned rocks
Along a littoral of bilge and horseshoe crabs,
A margin, a lull between the sea and the sand bluff
Crumbling into the sea, and saw the fishing boats
Trailing their lines of gulls, the tide pools' catch of shells,
And then the swallow's script (the figures it describes
In cursive, looping *o*'s and *u*'s, words caught on the wing)
Defining the cliff, like the madroñas and their exposed
Roots, the sallow stands of broom, the huddled couples . . .

Magnolia Bluff

This is a season and a place of small fruits;
Of curtains rinsed by the salt wind, and women
Sashaying down to the sea; of tripped alarms;
Of foxglove sending up its signal flares
For the men slumped on their steps or in their cars;
Of sparrows trellised to their feeders, swifts
Rising from the ashes on the bluff,
Gulls circling a yacht's bare masts, like hair;
Of sunstruck piano keys and loosened wires;
Of brass cannons, whitewashing, single sculls . . .

. . .

First, the pioneers misnamed the evergreens aligning and guarding the bluff.

Then workmen wove a fort around the madroñas, like a book's binding, and soldiers adopted the trees' point of view, aiming cannons at the Sound.

Gardeners combed the tangles out of the underbrush, loosening the madroñas' network of roots, the packed sand, the bluff. No one kept watch.

Soon the binding cracked. Another war broke out of its stall. The trees shed their bark and berries.

After the cannons were removed, and the deafened gunners returned to their pianos, realtors praised the view – schooners luffing into the wind and nets of oil, submarines and their tailings, the sheared mountains.

New families moved into the barracks and the houses back of the bluff. Seven madroñas sickened on the copper nails throbbing in their trunks, and died.

Meanwhile, the bluff continues to obey its own idea of scale, proportion, and timing, slipping out of its suits of macadam and broom, stripping itself of all its warning signs, scattering its trees, its footprints, according to a schedule no one can divine.

. . .

Suppose the abolitionists resurfaced
Here: if they revised their pamphlets and tactics
To fit these overseers, these shipbrokers
And lumbermen who build their houses up
On stilts, hoarding the bluff, the view, their tickets
To the last runs of salmon, fir, and oil,
And a civil war ensued; — would the man, the actor
Loading his silver-plated pistol, who wants
To close the show with a flourish, be discovered
In the wings — if not averted at the door?

. . .

It's time the barefoot scribes, the scavengers on the beach, found new shells for our legends — for the man cleaning his heart-shaped pool, dissolving the stains in the deep end, erasing memory; for the woman who changed her name and lowered her sights to half-mast; for the weedy crowd that thrives on arsenic draining into the sea . . .
    For the word sends its runners out again and again, each bearing a torch into the night:

All these antennas, these legislators of a dying race, lashed to our roofs and chimneys, centering our pictures of the walls between us,

While on the bluff a flayed madroña twists away from the road, toward the sea, awaiting its final conflagration.

. . .

At dusk, in the floodlit garden, a drunk slug
Weaves away from the fracas in the sunken pie tin, smudging
Lines of white dust, salt, and spittle, burning holes
In the skirts of marigolds. A Jacob's ladder
Shrivels on its wooden stakes, the laurel's in its cage
Of clippings, a cliff swallow's skimming insects off the top
Of the warm air. On the porch: glasses of curdled milk.
Someone looks up. Unfolds a map. Someone nods.
The lights dim. An F-16 beads together a string of clouds.
A black-sailed schooner tacks across the Sound.

Three Boats

Proud of its burden, the tugboat's a father
On the night shift, loading cement for his son
Who wants to be a singer or a priest;
An overseer watering his fields,
His daughters, and his slaves; a novelist
Leashed to his desk, wreathed in pipe smoke, and worn
Down by the words asleep on the last page,
Who groans, like the tug bellowing its horn
Until it finds the lane down which to tow
Its barge, its fruits, into the teeming harbor.

And the purse seine works in pairs — bride and groom,
Fence post and rail. It believes in cornerstones;
In sacraments of closure — eyelids, knots;
And in the woman following her husband
To another city and another set
Of circles to crack, islands to explore
And colonize before his lungs give out,
Before his creditors foul their air and water; —
Theirs is a marriage of necessity,
A balancing of nets, accounts, and soundings.

But the hydroplane delights in revelation.
Like the divine, it works in quick, sheer strokes;
Like money, it disappears before we know it.
It skims the Sound for the main points, ignoring
All the particulars — schooners, skiffs, kelp,
The buried reef; it scores the sheet of water,
Like a glass cutter, and then the sun applies
Its thumbprint till a window splits apart,
Revealing an old mariner and his secret
— The cache of emeralds hidden in the waves.

The Hurricane

As if a guest overturned the sea's glass tabletop, then made off with the buoys and floats, leaving the servants in a frenzy.

As if anyone could have stopped the surf, the tide's greedy heir, from wrapping the beach, the dunes, the whole island in winding sheets of sea wrack and foam.

Certainly no one on this partial list of retainers: mariners, fishermen, lifeguards, bodysurfers, sunbathers, scrimshawers, seascapists, weathermen, widows, walls . . .

Nor the sailors manning the warships perched on the horizon — birds tensed on a wire stretching around the world.

Nor even the evangelist bellowing in the television studio.

Not while sand swarmed up the road, clogging the exhaust pipes and engines of the cars and trucks headed for the mainland.

And over the canal the drawbridge opened, opened and swayed, its crossbars snapping like garters, its tender fleeing on foot.

And a bulkhead slid into the water, ripping off its salt-soaked planks,

Like an old lecher unbuttoning his coat, begging for release.

. . .

As if this uninvited guest despised our offerings — our weather maps and balloons, our sandbags and stilts, rickety stairways anchored in the dunes, rockets unleashed at the moon, barges spreading garbage all over the sea.

Because as hosts we had neglected our duties and thus upset the order of the universe.

An order we never understood nor successfully replaced.

For we couldn't waken from our sun-stunned drowse, couldn't tear ourselves away from the sand castle competition, the dune buggy races, the cockfights at the club.

Not even when the lifeguard raised the red flag, and saluted the storm clouds, and whistled in the swimmers and the end of summer.

Then the jetties, those long sleeves of rocks, gathered trawlers, steamers, and yachts, like lint.

And a sinking schooner wadded its sails, its handkerchiefs.

And the sea, mad dog, foamed at its mouth, this tidal inlet, then started chewing up the shore.

— All we could do was clap our hands . . . and wait for the help to come.

. . .

Yet there were those who called the hurricane a rite of passion, believing it would turn them in its four winds, would sweep their souls clean.

And some who tried to read its treatise nailed to the church door, while others prayed to learn where it got its marching orders and why it spurned our gifts.

And one who hoped its waves would hollow out the shells of words worn smooth on the lips of the crowd.

— They were the first to notice its open eye, the calm center of its fury.

But once the sand settled in the road, the skittish boats stopped straining to bolt from their slips and docks, and a boy, blinking away his mother's warning, scrambled up a dune to launch his kite.

A mote in the eye of a god, a surf-caster chuckled on his way to his favorite perch.

While an old man paced the vanishing shore, mumbling the names of all the women in his life.

Certain he could tame the winds gathering on the horizon.

— Then the eye closed, and the nightmare began again.

• • •

The summer houses propped up on the dunes, governments supported by a foreign power and subject to its shifting sense of priorities — toppled quickly, they embraced the harsh directives of wind and water, opening their doors and windows to the new order.

Like a coach with a drunken driver — that's how one cottage rode out to sea, spilling clothes, books, clocks, chairs, Persian rugs, and all the family secrets across the trail of a long high wave.

The same wave that towed abandoned cars up the canal and pushed a bungalow, like a baby stroller, across Dune Road then into Shinnecock Bay, where it stalled on an island of its own making.

A sandbar, really, with dashes of dune grass, macadam, stilts, and nails thrown in for support, around which a woman crazed by the winds would swim the next summer.

Singing, *There was a house, and then a hurricane* . . .

A place where the sun would rattle its keys and the conch shell own up to its white lies.

Where a poet learning to praise the winds might find a storm of words coming to rest.

Where lovers stranded on a reef of flesh and spirit could dream of making a fresh start.

Where the tide would slip in, like a familiar guest . . .

Scotch Broom: An Inventory

Sweeps salt air under the rug of the bluff.
Whisks sand and sunlight out of the rabbits' eyes.
When it snaps its pods, its hairy fingers, seeds gleam;
When it unlatches its doors, the winds take notice;
When it marches down the path, even horsetail shies.
It will stop at nothing to keep its job.

Like a cult, it colonizes barren places — cliffs,
Gravel-spattered hillsides, highway ditches and banks —
Then launches raids on our strongholds, our grazed fields
And woodlots. It sends its missionaries everywhere.
Red and yellow banners swirl in its parades.
Children recite its cribbed mythology.

Consider how easily it crossed the sea.
How long ago. How it seems to live on faith alone.
How it cloaks our barbed wire fences. And tucks
Our daggers up its sleeves. And chokes the revolution
In the grasses. How it will be the first
To claim our burned, our ravaged countrysides.

Early Poems

variation on a theme by Donald Justice

A thicket of softwoods — the scrub variety
Found on the upper slopes of mountains bordering
A desert — radiating from a single axis.
The first invaders after fire or a clear-cut,
Thus hollow-rooted and, after an initial spurt,
Slow-growing (except for the ones struck and scorched by lightning,
Which die, or surge above the others). Pliable,
Especially in the wind. Their bark scars easily.
Heals over. What's nesting in their branches? Solitaires,
Thrashers, jays — rival singers, imitators, and thieves.
Their leaves change color when the mule deer grow uneasy
And fall before the coneflowers, the exclamation
Points on a trail, have finished punctuating the wild.
Can stop an avalanche, stem floods, and offer shade
To seedlings. Sometimes give way to a stand of pines.

Lupines

for Agha Shahid Ali

This logging road could be in Appalachia
Or up the Amazon. And the search party, the ragged
Band of men outfitted with orange vests and field glasses
— Hunters, bird watchers, perhaps a survey crew . . .
Meanwhile, the man with the broken ankle
And his son, lost and hunkering along the ridge
Of this stripped mountain, are down to licorice sticks
And twigs. The man drifts in and out of sleep.
He keeps hearing wolves. There are lupines
Everywhere — blue, blue, and poisonous.
A chain saw gurgles across the valley, at the edge
Of the next clear-cut. In the distance, deer
And elk are returning to the sheared slopes of the volcano;
An ash plume hovers near the peak, like a debt.
No wolves in sight. Only a winter wren
Singing at the foot of a felled cedar, and over
The bowed heads of the searchers
In retreat a nighthawk steadying its wings for a glide,
A dive . . . On a houseboat in Kashmir, the father
Thinks in his delirium, a man's, a poet's
Tongue is turning black with ink; words fill the lake
Outside his door, like water lilies
Opening at daybreak, or like the lupines,
The wolfbeans his son is begging him to eat. *Eat.*

Exiles

We stole the comet from the Planetarium,
Soaked our clothes in creosote, stuffed the mailbox
With rattlers — anything to stop those circulars!
Then we clipped the police notes from the newspaper, planning
The perfect crime. We ate well. Slept soundly. Rose late.
We were an easy mark for traveling salesmen.
We bought brushes, chocolate bars, maps of India;
Encyclopedias lined our walls, like plates of armor.
We became a captive audience. The Festival
Of Saints, no less than the forests burning in the West,
We praised until our throats were raw. We loved nightfall,
Loved stoking the wood stove with our checkbooks and receipts,
And loosening our belts before each meal. The comet?
We hung it from the rafters and took aim. Then we lit
Matches, and brought them to our lips, and made a wish.

Jaime Sabines: From *Lost Birds*

III.
I'm hungry. I need to fast.

VII.
They say you're a mess because they're used to gardens, not jungles.

IX.
In the quiet of the afternoon the shadows of the trees play hide-and-seek, like the shadows in my heart.

XII.
God's secret: He put his lips to my ear and didn't say a thing.

XIV.
The sting of the butterfly is worse than a snakebite.

XV.
How should you write "water"? Wah, wah-ter . . . like a thirsty man.

XVI.
I'm sick of poets and debutantes. They're always rehearsing for their debut.

XVII.
The mouse complained about his cage: I can stand the wheat, the bread crumbs, the kernels of corn. What I can't take is this oppression, this darkness.

XVIII.
The perfect crime would be a suicide that looks like a murder. Someday I'll shoot myself in the back.

XX.
They told me about marijuana, heroin, mushrooms, peyote. That's

how they found God, became perfect, disappeared.

But me, I prefer my old hallucinogens: solitude, love, death.

XXV.

The flies explode in the heat. There's a humming of black petals, a pecking in the air, skins smeared with honey, slow stupid hours in the same place. The flies give off heat, quiet black drops of heat. Among their thousand feet the heat explodes.

XXVII.

The beautiful blank page! Like a naked woman, waiting. First an invitation, then a calling, then urgency, fate. All love is writing, inscription.

XXXI.

I might have found you ten years earlier or ten years later. But you got here just in time.

XXXII.

I took off my shoes to walk on the coals.
I took off my skin to wrap around you.
I took off my body to love you.
I took off my soul to be you.

XXXVII.

What's the difference between the two or three days of the fly and the two hundred years of the turtle?

Doppelgänger

The man who called and wanted my wife's measurements;
Who sent me to the closet, the bureau, and the trunk,
Gathering clothes like a stockboy; who took away
Her favorite colors, her pants' length, the cut of her bra —
For a surprise; who claimed he had a photograph;
Who said she was carrying his child; who needed her,
Like me; who promised not to hurt her, like me; whose lines
Of speech blurred in the wake of passing cars and sirens;
Whose name kept changing, like the weather and the leaves;
Who said we'd talk again; who refused to say goodbye;
Who's hidden now among these words; who tilts my pencil
Toward the ocean and the sky, still writing, *Are you there?*

Laments

At sunrise, on Mt. Aire, my wife's beside herself
Again. Ours is the stubborn grief of a rock climber
Stopped by an overhang – thick rope; click of the wind;
The granite ticking underfoot . . . Once more we gauge
The length and look of our dispute. These are familiar
Notes, a song in common time: the calluses,
The scars, the drop-off, finger- and footholds, the peak.
One step. Another . . . No. What can we do but sing?

. . .

September 10th, and one skyrocket on a stem
Of spent shells, a charge leftover from the summer's war –
I note the way this burst of scarlet hangs in the air;
And how the scrub oaks split or swell around the stones
Embedded in their trunks – the pearls woodcutters harvest;
And why she lingers by the stream, tracing a set
Of initials carved into a quaking aspen: the bark
Is healing over, blurring the letters and the date.

. . .

Let's say we're saxifrage and rock – "A Sort of a Song,"
As Williams twanged, praising invention . . . But if we break
The habit of our grief? I'll say the moon became
A dried cork stoppering a bottleful of dust –
The last of the night's reserves. That mist was in the canyon,
Waiting for the old sun to sidle up to the ridge
And send it home. That we were lost. Frightened. Alone.
Then a crumbling wall, and in the crevices: flowers.

. . .

A slashed rattler stiffens on the trail, headless,
Tailless, worked over with a shovel or a knife —
A souvenir hunter's debris. Uncoiled and tied
To nothing, it's a rope whose ends were burned to keep
The hemp from fraying, a rope which shed its knots and slipped
From the piton's eye, then slid like a tear down the face
Of the rock, splattering the trail we hike half-blind.
Vandals, beware: a snake's head, dead and bagged, can still strike.

. . .

What I'll remember of our argument is autumn's
Wreckage: the aspens loosening their hold on the steep,
The clear-cut gashes stitched together with their roots;
Mules-ears corralled and tanned by the sun; the ratcheting
Of squirrels in the pines, turning the season's wheels;
A dry creek, and monkshood on the ground, folding
Its garments up; mascara furrowing her cheeks;
My words, my anger cascading down the mountainside . . .

. . .

Now on the summit overlooking Parley's Canyon,
The city, the interstate: How will this end? I ask.
No answer . . . Too tired to keep fighting, we watch the cars
Heading for the pass; and when we turn away, we find
A marten in a seethe. A pika needling
Into its haystack bleats and bleats. A rock wren bobs.
Then a locust rattles out of sleep, and our shadows lengthen
Toward the city, like snakes uncoiling in the heat.

Autumn Sequence

Indian summer in a posted field —
Here's the stubble where the lovers adrift
On a float of folded jeans and sweaters ignore
The hounds circling the neighbor's field, like a fence,
Whistles and birdcalls, shotguns testing the air . . .
Screened by a raveling skirt of corn, the lovers
Sigh, and wriggle along the earth, and listen
For the whir and hum of beating wings, the prelude
To the songs of the pheasants, grouse, and partridges,
Which must also find protected fields.

. . .

A night-long riot of wet snow and wind
And branches breaking, tearing the lines down . . .
This leaf-laden crowd of sugar maples bows
Under the weight of its own history,
While the sycamore's fruit plunks into the rough
And slush of the sidewalk, like yellow golf balls —
Winter rules today. A willow bleeds;
The sumac bending over backwards cramps,
Locks; in a cold dark house a couple bickers —
They search for candles, matches, they do not touch.

. . .

This, then: her splintered shoulder pinned and wedged
Apart, her back a maze of metal braces,
Her spindled legs raised overhead (to calm
Her fluttering heart, framing the sky in a V),
The widow on the lawn chair reads a book
Of manners in the felled oaks and foul wind
Until she spots geese in their lines — and the notes
That fill those lines, the blurring hieroglyphs
Of their migration. Drawing in her legs,
Heart flapping, she rises with them, almost singing.

Immanent

for Brewster Ghiselin

When the wind spackling the flower beds
With flyleaves, broken branches, and weed seeds
Picks up and brushes on its sleet and snow,
Sealing crocuses in their catacombs,
Like schooners dry-docked in a frozen harbor,
The hoary mariner in his widow's walk
May examine the stretched canvas of the sea
And find — to his chagrin — a single star
Revolving over the deep: the lighthouse beam.

. . .

Here's driftwood lifted and laid by on the shore,
Salt-bleached, riddled with sand fleas, kelp, and tar,
A sheaf of cavities and empty lines
To be unloaded in the studio,
Where the cat stretching in the moonlight will scratch it
Down to its roan and russet skins and manes,
Leaving a galaxy of flecks on the floor
From which new constellations may appear —
A headless horseman, a rowboat, scales, threads . . .

. . .

Though autumn leaves its tear sheets by the road
For the proofreaders in the tour buses;
And a woman flies to the Caribbean,
Prepared to dive for a shipful of bones
Buried in a reef; and a galley slave goes mad,
Jumps overboard, and then returns to his freighter; —
Here in this inland city, where salted wood
Burns in the grates, charring the map of the sky,
Bulbs in their harbors raise their sails and make way.

Old Wives' Tales

The star moss constellating in the woods
Is a green heaven for the grubs and newts,
The fiction and stage set governing the movements
Of the toad stalled in its eccentric orbit,
Eclipsed by the waning shadows, the leaf mold,
Waiting for the hikers to pass — *Look: a toad!*

. . .

There was a quiet boy who placed a toad
Like a wafer on his tongue: no priest or doctor
Could explain his scizures, and the old wives' tale stops
At warts, a partial account, like the tears of the girl
Who pushes her stepfather's sweaty hand
Away — what fable can account for *that?*

. . .

Here, said the widow, wrapping the child's thumb
In a silk scarf, *those nasty little warts*
Will disappear in a week — and so they did . . .
And as for the children sleeping on the swings?
Their mothers wrote their nicknames in the sand,
Kissed them, and left — or so one story goes . . .

. . .

The child siphoning words out of the books
Inverted on the shelves in his father's study —
He's stealing fuel for his escape: ink burns
His tongue and eyes . . . Where will he hide? In books?
Or in the mica mine, where his words may light
The mirrors falling from the walls, like leaves?

. . .

I love the way these cultivars *escape* —
Broom, cockatoos, the model slumming, lines
Which stray and hide their measure from the boxed
And blinded writer cleaning off his desk,
The canyon stream flooding the retaining walls
To carve in the road and aspens its initials . . .

. . .

Consider the gang that razed the aviary,
Tore wings (like stamps) off the exotic geese,
Doused them in lighter fluid, then struck a match —
Who can predict what course a child will take?
The weather's easier: lightning anchoring
The clouds, the storm rowing around the valley . . .

. . .

Ordered to burn the Northwest's forests down,
The old men, women, and children of Japan
Launched weather balloons packed with blasting powder
And caps to cross the Pacific, following
The labyrinthine thread of the Gulf Stream,
A flock of tinders on its fall migration.

. . .

Water's my will, and my way, the poet sang,
Charting his spirit's motion in and out
Of the waves, interpreting his purl and babble
As tides, snail song, a widow's rasp . . . Unmoored
And tangled in his nets, he sank and sank,
Words lighting his waters, like a diver's lamp.

. . .

Where did I get these words? asked the apprentice.
He learned them from the toad that sent him spinning
Like a comet, coaxing poems from his seizures,
As a gardener trains a gnarled grape vine to grow
In lines along a fence, twisting its tendrils
Into an ornament, which may bear fruit.

. . .

A blaze of snow singeing the grass, marking
Trails through the sycamores; a shock of white
Reeds stacked against the fence; a sheaf of papers; —
Thus the eye works through an October squall,
Harvesting light instead of fruit, arranging
The clouds into a pattern it can use.

. . .

Rained out: the enemy's timber-burning plan.
Yet a family mushrooming in the Cascades
Found a tin can, a sodden charge, which flashed
Like a peacock's train, a falling star . . . The censor
Buried the news in their obituaries:
A Hiking Accident . . . There will be others.

. . .

These Buddhist students of America
Vowing to make their vows in Japanese —
They chant the foreign syllables, like a deaf
Poet mangling the music of his lines,
Or a priest intoning Latin, another language
He may not understand nor care to learn.

• • •

It's not enough to *think* these pockmarked hills
Can be restored . . . Scribes of the spirit's absence,
Who will sign your paychecks when the words
Rot in your journals of the self? A poem
Must declare its independence, like the elm
Spared from the diseased crowd, the stumped horizon.

• • •

The radiator cleared its throat, and the living
Room stood at attention for the bookish man,
Who saw familiar words, like *indigenous*
And *et cetera,* catch in the net of iron
Gills, become salmon thrashing in the locks,
And spawn new words: *kingfisher, avatar. . .*

• • •

What shall we call that constellation of spy
Satellites hanging from Orion's Belt,
Like keys? Is it the Janitor who works
For the guardians and gaugers of our sleep,
Pushing his spangled broom down nightmare's halls?
Or the Hunter with another scorpion?

• • •

Now the words glide, like skates, over the pages
Of the man who rose at daybreak, praying for clear
Weather and words with which to carve a figure
For his joy and grief: the boy who skated alone
On the pond in the woods, his hockey stick the rudder
For his rushes up and down the melting ice.

Grace

In the collapsed veins of the leaves
Lining the path, like mourners; in the procession
Of firs bearing the sky to its final resting place;
And in the snow falling at dusk, covering
The footsteps of burglars and brides; — in each moment,
Death hangs its gloves from another nail, and grace,
In a white robe, flares on the horizon: a shooting star.

The Greenhouse

Three racks of unused seeds, a spill of poisoned water
Sweeping the floor, flats laid out on a table, like coffins —
Has it begun again? The emptying of pockets?
The braiding of flags with fists? There's a woman
With rubber gloves, a man in a black vest. She wants
A healthy child, he wants the straggling fuchsias
Trimmed to their wicks. *Some men like dancing,* she thinks.
What happened to the saw? he asks himself. *To summer?*

Outside, in the windstorm, uprooted fruit trees
Float in place, unloading their leaves, their cargo
And commands; hooded traffic signals, like hanged men, swing;
The bridge weighs anchor, the bridge sails away; —
What have we done? There's a woman in galoshes,
A man with a white tie. She'd like to pan for gold,
He dreams of opening a bar. *Luck,* she whispers, *opens*
Doors like the wind. No one ever enters, he mutters, *or leaves.*

And then? A swirl of sawdust, a rattle of racks.
The fuchsia's steady flame. That sweet smell rising
From the floor, and hundreds of eyes opening in the flats; —
And yet, and yet . . . There's a woman rubbing her hands, a man
Adjusting his spats. She hopes the orchids bloom, the treated
Holly lasts. He needs to clear the branches from the roof.
When the clocks ran in place, she reminds him at the door.
When the clocks stopped, he sighs — and they did, they do.

The Haven

Where a fir leans over the trail, snow-pitched,
Wind-notched, wedged between today
And tomorrow in the top branches of an aspen,
One of the ancients slumped in a stranger's arms,

Its burst roots buried under the stairway
Of a whitened hummock, its needles
Filling both ski tracks, both pairs of lines
Imprinted in the waxed and melting snow —

This is where I stop
And listen to the skins of ice hanging from the canyon walls
Stretch and crack in the sun; to the dipper's song
As it slips into the creek

And starts its long march upstream and underwater;
And to the iced mugs of reeds and rushes
Clinking in the wind, in a toast to the end
Of winter, while a SAC bomber rakes and seeds the airways; —

This is where I wait for you.

Winterings

for James Galvin

Sentences unrolling like slatted fences, catching the flocks and drifts of language buried in the snow's blank slate.

When the front skids to a stop, the first wet flakes glister the grave-yard road and wipe the headstones clean.

In the boarded-up school: a squall of chalk dust, white spiders in a glide down the web of the window, inkwells erupting in the covered desks.

A galaxy of bright green globes revolves around the apple tree until the snow slips off the leaves, like falling stars.

The yew's cocoon exploding in the wind: hundreds of white butter-flies rend the air, descending slowly, covering our tracks.

A thin glaze shrouds the frozen lake, where boys learn to skate around the holes grief leaves – lost pucks, light, words and words: the ruined sheen.

André Breton

"Je cherche l'or du temps."
— from his obituary notice

At nightfall, when the plowman and the pianist
Collided in the street, and the clothesline stretched, snapped,
The coffee tree, with its sheaths clipped to its bare limbs
And sparrows riffling through its knives and seeds, became
An emblem for the season, an audience of one —
Black ice, white sheets, the tone-deaf singer on his knees:

Gold coursed through the collapsing veins of his last words.

A Primer

As for the existence of a secret tradition? Everyone was anxious to speak to me. Yet silver coins, like children, continued to roll down the hills and into the streets. Marching bands circled the draining pond. Soldiers staked off the boundaries of the sky. Thus I traveled to the hinterland, where I found only sandstone and sage. I lay in the sun until my skin blistered. Then I heard the drums of the cliff dwellers who vanished centuries ago . . .

• • •

The station, it's true, had fallen into disrepair. Every night, in the same truck, a different set of thieves arrived to cart away the bricks. Soon nothing was left but a halo of cinders surrounding the foundation. When fireweed sprouted along the sidewalk, the couple that used to argue in the building across the street moved into a house of their own. (His business in wooden ducks being brisk that fall, they could afford to have her tubes tied, too.)

• • •

Nevertheless, no one knows when the train disappeared, what you were planning to order before we walked in, or if the season will ever end. Even now the cemetery is a wash of plastic flowers and hungry deer reluctant to return to the hills. Even now there are fortunes to be made. The abandoned saltworks, for example: How could you have known they would come to mean so much today? And the fences? Build them along here, and here, and here . . .

• • •

A new time signature is what we need, not more historians bent on updating and expanding *The Lives of the Saints*. Modulations in the weather – the way fog rises from melting snow, the number of traffic accidents averted thanks to the increased use of headlights, the precise moment sap begins to ooze through the veins of the girdled maple — will always be recorded, though the key remains the same: *winter.*

. . .

And if in the course of opening and closing our doors and magazines, of drawing the curtains against the street lamps' glare, a note of surprise — an unexpected guest — should wander into our quiet conversation and lead us not into temptation but up into the canyon, where the headwaters of the spring floods are gathering material, like a biographer — don't take that to mean the schedule has changed. Not yet, anyway.

Lines on the Vernal Equinox

Now, at daybreak, the snow-crowned mountains gleam;
And in the tawny hills, where iced buds crack and swell
And mist slips over the deer and elk, as though to hide them
From the hounds baying in the valley, the sun's a hunter.
Now the black-capped chickadees begin their two-note hymns,
Transposing keys as they see fit; — and now the sleepers,
The lovers trapped in their argument, rise. Rise and shine.

Excerpts from a Commonplace Book

. . . And Sorrow with her family of Sighs
Visited again last night, strewing
Their hats and threadbare coats across the floor,
Complaining to the wind about the wine
And the violin — and then, like refugees,
They huddled on the bulging trunks, smoking
And waiting for a train to take them away,
Refusing our commands and cries to leave.

. . .

The dying aspen leans against the sky,
Straightening its new leaves; haloes of ash
Bead the rain-soaked furrows prepared for sun
And seed; a flicker drums on the drainpipe; —
Now all is pattern, all is form, and those nights
In the hayloft haunt me, love: How will we find
The ladder and the light again? And why
Did the horses remain silent in their stalls?

. . .

A freight train abandoned in the desert,
Its engines locked at either end, the keys
To the new cars adrift in the bursar's drawer,
Fruits and vegetables steamed in their crates to a pulp,
Dried milk incrusting the insides of the tankers
Like salt, a hobo exploding in a boxcar,
Coal dust returning to its element,
And the wind raising all its hands to help.

Presswork

Then the retreat of glacier lilies up the mountain,
Their sheets of gold withdrawing from spring's fray, like gilding
Stripped from a palace, hammered into coin, and spent
By the new guard, the mule deer stubbling the steep,
Carving their paths behind these blooms, like melting glaciers.

. . .

The mountain's spine cracked in the heat and heave, and let
Another sheaf of boulders fly . . . No thread can hold
Those folios forever, which is why the rocks
Cascading over the holly-grapes and horsemint settled
In the scree field by the lake — and why these words are here.

. . .

A stone cleaved into thirds. The broadax wriggling
Out of its handle, its stiff clothes. These last scrub oaks,
Like a thicket of stopped clocks. The finger exercises
Of wind in the chimes. The grass, a harbor for the arks
Of rain. The lovers in their cages, testing their wings.

April

A line of glacier lilies engraved in snow.
An ash- and soot-stained aspen rinsed with catkins.
The red-tailed hawk patrolling the cliff and sky.

All winter, while I tried to strip the ledger
Boards from my fences and handrails, the signs
By which you know me now, I sang to no one,

Not even you, love, keeper of the hymns . . .

A woman runs along the swollen creek.
A butterfly unfurls its flag in the road.
The old words lift their heavy wings, and fly.

Because

variation on a theme by Yannis Ritsos

Because the Dead Sea released its hostages — the taste for salt, a
    rudder and a sail;
Because a band of Roman slaves, disguised in their master's robes,
    fled across the Continent;
Because one manuscript, one waxen shoal of words, burned a
    monastery down;
Because the sun spurned the Black Forest, and windmills ground the
    peasants into the earth, into the air, into the voice of the boy
    who cried wolf;
Because the crowd hissed at the empty stage, and the prompter
    drank himself to sleep, and the diva hid in the pit;
Because we let barbed wire replace our wooden faces and fences;
Because a scream left a trail through the ruined air;
Because I followed that trail into the woods, where my hands
    dissolved in smoke and rain;
Because I wandered for days, weeks, until I found himself outside
    a walled city, a city abandoned hundreds of years ago;
Because I couldn't scale the walls nor find a way to return to my
    homeland, and so I settled along a river in the desert;
Because the river changed course, and its banks crumbled into the
    dry bed, where I was on my knees, speechless and afraid;
Because whenever I hike into the desert, I talk and talk and talk;
Because I have never been to the desert;
Because I refuse to follow any trail whose markings are not com-
    pletely clear;
Because I distrust signs, guideposts, land- and seamarks;
Because on my single visit to the ancient city I rifled the ruins for
    potsherds and stone tools — and was warned never to return;
Because I heed all warnings, all directives from the crowd;
Because I won't listen to anyone but myself;
Because I love to cry wolf;

Because everything I read smells of smoke;
Because sometimes I wake at night to find my hands covered with
    salt, my sheet wrapped around me like a sail;
Because I can't tell if this is the desert or the sea;
Because I never learned to read the stars and don't know where
    we're heading;
Because of this and more, much more, I hid your name in the well . . .
    and here it is again, filling my cup.

LUCK

Lucky *and* unlucky *mean the same thing,*
like flammable *and* inflammable.
— William Matthews

Erosion

"Parachuting into the desert is a quiet arrival,
but I've seen hillsides become alive with snakes."
— Dr. Gerald Crenshaw, *Albuquerque Journal*

Past the salt flats, the grave of the sea, the sky
Divers in a free fall, twisting and turning,
Like stones dropped in water — they heard only the whine
Of the wind, the drone of the plane flying home.

Their chutes erupted like an argument,
And up they floated, up — then down. They saw smoke
Rising from the last city, houses reclining
On the worn benches of the mountains, and rain

Evaporating in midair. They carried
Their own clouds into the desert, the rippling
Cloth and cords trailing them like debts, like children
And beliefs. And once they landed on the mesa,

Splashing into the sand, they felt the past
Dissolve. So they praised the action of their chutes
Settling, like snow, over the stunted trees,
Over all the shrubs and flowers they would have

To name. They praised the ebbing wind, the silence,
And the taste of their own salt. They praised a cactus
In the shape of a cross . . . Yet it was a dead place
To these disciples of the future, these

Pilgrims gathering potsherds and petrified
Chunks of wood. They damned the dry gullies. Damned
The heat rooted in the red earth and the hidden
Barbs of the prickly pear . . . Then it began.

In arroyos, on hillsides: a hissing and
A heaving, like the sea. Or was this just
The memory of the sea? They waved at the sky,
They scanned birds' nests, gopher holes, anthills, ants:

Nothing. One laced up his boots. Another grabbed
A hatchet. A third tried to pray. Soon waves
Of diamondbacks were breaking on the mesa,
Eroding the shore beneath the nomads' feet.

Dog, Howling

Our neighbor's Seeing Eye
Dog's on the dole and going
Blind, mocking his master,
The piano tuner. A trusting
German shepherd turned out
To sleep in the garage,
A police dog slobbering
On his beat — terrified
Of the dark, he leads a chorus
Of Airedales and Dobermans,
The canyon's guardians,
In a nightly round of howls.

What sets him off? The coyote
In the apple orchard,
Finishing off the fallen
Fruit? The horse splintering
Its stall, then kicking its trough,
Its supply of straw and ice?
The poacher at the end
Of the dirt road, who trains
His headlights on a startled doe?
Something from memory —
A crosswalk? a jangling upright?
An abandoned baby grand?

Or is he simply howling
At the hunter's moon, that rag
Ranchers used to clean
These hills, scrubbing off
The rabbits and the wolves?

Here's what I know:
The rattlesnakes are in their dens,
Asleep. Our neighbor's retired,
Knows what parts of town
To avoid after dark, and likes
His new cane. Once I open
The door, the noise will stop.

The Sirens

*"Most of the people I listen to are either dead
or Brazilians."*
                                    — Dave Frishberg

He took his bearings from the black keys, the pianist
In search of the essential, the spare, this man
Who had left everything behind — charts,
Scores, clubs and concert halls, sopranos and summers
By the sea . . . He wore white gloves and a watch cap.
He walked without a limp. There was still time to dismantle
The TV, the radio. Time to collect his books
Into cardboard boxes and hide them outside
The governor's mansion. Time even
To bale newspapers with piano wire, then drop them off
The drawbridge . . . The mail? Forwarded
To his favorite critic, Madame X. To the Red Cross
Went the spoils of his endless war
On silence — records, tapes, the telephone, a summons
To appear at the local nursing home . . . He locked his windows
And doors. He sat at the piano, listening.

It wasn't long before they started, the voices
Of the dead, his dead, and oh,
How they resembled music . . . from Brazil!
A music and a language full of mists and mangoes,
Broad savannahs and sacks of coffee beans.
He heard no humming from the French composer
Huddling in the trenches, in the Great War,
Those melodies persistent as shelling
And the taste of mustard gas. Nor could he remember
The way that clarinetist slid up the scale,
Sure-fingered as a boy scrambling
To the top of a greased pole, daring the orchestra
And audience to follow him, to catch in his glissando

Sight of the ocean and the sky . . . No.

Now he was with the *Great Invisibles,*
Translating into lines and bars and Portuguese
Snatches of their constant hum and murmur. Bow makers
And the bossa nova, sierras and seamstresses,
Cattle drovers and casino chips —
How quickly they assumed the mantle of the dead!
How lovely they had grown! In his mother's warnings
He heard the work songs of women washing clothes
Along the Amazon; his father's threats
Became the hymns and chants of men
Who carry anacondas. And he was in a river boat,
Wedged between a poet and a nun, heading up a nameless
Tributary to listen to the river spirits, their water music
— Or was this Carnival? And who were all
These dancers, these painted men and women emerging
From his memory? What sambas did they know?

His brother skipped out of a crowded trolley
— A thief, a sideman and squanderer of perfect pitch,
A tireless junketeer who had called Nowhere
Home. Who had disappeared in Rio. His dirty jokes
Were the jingles of a squatter's child
Set loose on the streets sinking in the rain. Then a woman
Came, in sequins and leather boots, raising her finger
To accuse, conduct, or beckon — the pianist
Couldn't say. What did he know? Her tears were fire
Balloons drifting through the night, lighting
Her father's orange grove; her name
Escaped him, like the flames spiraling toward the stars.
And finally his idol, the one-armed trumpeter
On a run, in a drunken blur of notes
Bearing no resemblance to the rhapsodies the nervous
Pianist had transcribed in his youth, shuffled off the stage
Of a cafe he had never seen before — and that was where

He smelled the fabled *perfumes of Brazil!*

He began to tremble: like tango music,
Like the rhythm of the rumba, Portuguese
Had been another language to ignore. Yet here he was
Scribbling in his composition book words netted in the sea
Off the coast of São Paulo – *dançavam, cantavam,*
Dormido . . . Salt was on his lips,
And he kept rising to his feet, reaching for the missing
Singers, the sirens he had avoided in his desire
To translate all his questions, every noise
And silence into song. How could he block them out?
How could anyone refuse this calling?
He vowed not to turn away again, for he had wanted
To listen to his own inflections . . . only to discover
These voices were all he had, voices whose pitch and timbre
Had always tuned his speech, memory, dreams
– Music to accompany him the rest of the way: *Where*
Were you when we needed you? cried his mother,
What was so important? asked his father.
My name's Maria, said the woman in sequins. *Please remember.*

Sunset. And light staining the windows.
And clouds withdrawing their claims on the sky. This was
– This had been his brother's favorite time of day,
Of year. There were leaves matted on the roof,
Covering wires, as if to hide a nest of hibernating snakes.
Camellias arranged in their annual display,
Their waxworks of white and crimson blossoms. Two robins
Bobbing to each other on the sidewalk, obeying
Amenities beyond his comprehension.
An old man waved a cut and supple wand
Of forsythia, gilding the dormant grass . . . The pianist
Took his seat and, raising his hands, surrendered
To the voices multiplying in his ear,
Voices he no longer recognized. Nor would he forget them.

These singers, these spirits summoned from his past,
Voices forged out of all his chance encounters
— They were here to stay. Thus he realized
His work would never end — the work of honoring
The dead, of salving with his music
Nerves raveled by the swelling racket of the age,
The din that forced these spirits into speech and song,
Prompting him to listen like a servant,
To attend . . . Something would remain unfinished.

Soon the shadows slipped out of their moorings. Vanished.
Tides churned in the drawn nets of the moon.
And in the Bering Sea a century wave
Prepared to swamp a fishing fleet — another skirmish
In an ancient war . . . Here in the gathering
Darkness, where the steady flaring
Of the metronome resembled the revolutions
Of a lighthouse beam, the pianist could almost believe
He was at sea. His legs were rubbery, and his music rippled
Away from him, washing over the walls and windows.
Propped against the sky was the rungless ladder stars
And sailors climb into the night . . . There were
No other islands to explore, nor horizons
Tempting him to stray. Only new scales to memorize, charts
To distribute to the poor and homeless,
And scores to settle for the sirens
Haunting him in a dozen different tongues . . . Good weather
Was in the offing, and he foresaw nothing
To waylay him. Through the long night he kept watch.

(In memory of Elizabeth Bishop and Carlos Drummond de Andrade)

Breath

for Stephen Dunn

Does it imagine it's a world
Unto itself — the blowfish caught
And kept out of the rank canal,
The puffer drying like a sheet
On the boy's ten-pound test? Inspect
The evidence, the boy believes.
And asserts, sputtering at the sky,
Twirling his catch, like a tetherball.

How it gulps the salt air, thirsty
For home; gnaws at the shank of the hook
Anchored in its lip, sharpening
Its pair of teeth against the wire;
Adapts to anything, this brash
Believer in itself, bobbing
Like a buoy in a storm — even
To the spit and tickling of the boy.

Who's seen them floating belly-up
Around the slip, as if dead — bankrupts
Fooling their creditors; and having
Baited his hook for weakfish or flounder,
Cast his line into the oily
Wake of a pleasure boat, and reeled
In what he thought would be his lunch,
He's tempted to unmask this fraud.

To prick the skin of this balloon
Launched from the deep. And hear the pop
Or hiss of air escaping . . . But won't:
Why risk bad luck? For this defender

Of the dark and marvelous, which swells
In the light, billows in the wind,
And is the wind ensnared and salted,
Changing direction, shape, and hue,

Frightens him. He wonders why
In death it must secrete its poison
In the sweet meat the Japanese
Serve their guests, sometimes killing them,
And what that says about his world?
Someday, reading a poem, he'll learn
The blowfish is a delicacy
— And dangerous, like poetry . . .

Now he sighs. Cuts the line. Soon
A yacht chugs past, sails down, its wake
Surging and spilling into the slip,
And on its deck a woman bronzing
In a bikini stretches, turns,
Her breasts flopping out of her top,
Stunning the boy, who holds his breath
And starts to count, backwards from ten.

Coastlines

That inland sea whose coastlines keep expanding,
That ancient ocean in which nothing lives
Save the brine shrimp culled for aquariums
And skittering on its surface hordes of flies
Hoarding our slackening attention, that thought
Which swelled with mountain runoff until it swamped
Sailboats and railroad tracks, saltworks and roads,
Still rises since the foothills stripped of timber
Hold nothing back — snowmelt, and mud, and rancor.

Why did I dismiss the warning signs —
The flooded pastures and abandoned farms,
Convicts filling sand bags, tall mounds of tires
Burning each night on the salt flats, a pack
Of flames emerging from the test site's craters,
The revelations of the reinless ghosts
Who raveled the shoreline and whose descendants
Are moving even now to higher ground?
I, too, believed we would escape the flood.

. . .

Another rut of restaurants in "weathered" wood
— A zoning law mechanical as meter
And blind as the men who colonized this coast,
The dreamers who portioned out the shore, building
The bungalows that lined the beach, the diners
And sad motels sunbathers blistered in,
The trinket shops whose clerks were on the take . . .
All gone. And this uniform, this battleship
Grey, which rhymes with almost everything —
The bank, the church, gas stations, galleries —
Lacks the color of the clouds, and the pilings,
And the salt-eaten, sea-bleached cottages

Pocking the hills beyond the town, which weathered
Another winter of high winds and waves,
And which draw us here again to heal ourselves,
Like spindrift draining back into the sea.

. . .

These oil-slicked and foaming sea anemones
Pulsing in the tide pools, in the outriding
Wash of the waves — did they survive the spill?
Or did they migrate here after the cleanup?

We can't tell. And the boundaries of this cove,
The boulders and stumps of driftwood streaked with black
Gold, issue of the foreign tanker that foundered
Off the coast, will give no answers; riddled
By sun and wind and water, studded with clumps
Of barnacles, then sealed with seaweed, they make
Only a pair of headlands, where salt spray hangs
Like a net spread and drying on the sand,
Or like the film of oil that coated, clotted
The water, killing gulls, and crabs, and the sea
Anemones . . .
                    Why are you crying, love?
Why cry when you can see they will survive —
Patina green, oil-cast, and almost still
As statues weathering the elements?

. . .

We say a solvent man's good for his debts.
Likewise, the woman soaking her stained skirt
In gasoline, the young wife studying
Her husband's mail: believers in redemption.
Moonshine, and money, and counseling: solvents all.
And all inflammable, given the right

Conditions — a slick road, a rush on silver,
A smudge that won't come out . . .
                        Remember the man
Who promised not to bother anyone?
Who wrapped a beach towel dipped in stolen ether
Around his head and slept for sixteen hours?
He could have blown his house into the sea.

And he dreamed of nothing, though dreams are solvents, too.
They're what distinguish the lovers on the boardwalk
From the developers surveying the hills,
The bankrupt merchants, and the men in turbans —
Distinguish and unite, just as the moon
Working in concert with the tides will light
And loosen the shrubs and trees along the bluff
Before it drags them down into the water.

. . .

Daybreak, and the dead weight of memory
Hanging . . .
            like a black eel hooked in its side
And dangling from the fishing line of a boy
Whose luck surprises him and who believes
He's reeling in seaweed, a sunken buoy,
Perhaps a fisherman's torn net or boot —
Imagine his amazement when he finds
A bloodied eel wriggling to the surface
Of the canal, writhing into the salt air,
Its mouth ripped open by a motorboat.

What balances memory, if not the tilt
And lift of the imagination as it lights
The buried scene? Listen: I was that boy.
And this morning, on another coast, I rose
From a dream in which I caught that eel again

And once more cut my line to let it die
Or heal itself down in the deep. Then I turned
To see you had been crying in your sleep.

. . .

And here's the boy adrift in a borrowed dinghy
Who, having wrapped his sail around the mast,
Must work the rudder like an oar, rowing
Nowhere, in a half-circle, back and forth
Among the whitecaps rumpling the cove,
Now yawing toward the salt marsh and submerged
Rocks that bulwark the shore, now cursing his luck,
Cursing the boys from the yacht club, the sailors
Who snubbed or swamped him in the public race
(And have already moored their catamarans
To the floats across the water and gone home).

Yet once the rudder cracks, and he discovers
He can no longer will his little boat
To stay in place, he may unfurl his sail
And learn to tack, to jibe and come about,
Submitting to the dictates of the wind,
Zigzagging toward the buoys, then the bay,
The choppy inlet, and finally the sea.

. . .

What wrack, what spoils the beach divided up
Only to let another tide reclaim them:
The pulp of seaweed stretched out on the shore
And drying into strips of paper – shredded
Journals no one could read; the mail and armor
Torn from a dying horseshoe crab and cast
Off by its nameless conqueror; the sand
Dollars and other forms of currency

144

Beachcombers hoarded – trinkets of seaglass
Unsuited to the gift shop trade, starfish
Stiffening in a slow burn, like the myths
Of the gods constellated in the skies,
Conches and their false depths; the mussel shells
Picked clean and then discarded, like billfolds
And letters censors open for inspection;
The icebox washed out in a hurricane,
Dragged back in a spring tide, and settling
Into the sand, like a beached whale; the oil
Spill ribboning the shore in bands of black
And white, like a keyboard for the sun to play,
Pounding the dark notes harder than the light
– Where I would run all summer as a child
With one foot in each world, singing *Hot, cool,*
Hot, daring them to blend into one chord . . .

. . .

What else remains? The singe, the sear, the way
A rusted spike burned through my bare foot, fusing
The beach, dried seaweed, and the driftwood plank
I'd stumbled down (manacled in my sprint
Away from home) and off into a swell
Of sand, which turned the crimson of the sky
Awakening sailors dread; and as my blood
Ebbed in its poisoned tide, my childhood nailed
Itself in place, securing for these pages
The prospect of that morning by the sea:

Rumors of sharks and submarines, of riptides
And calm; the bonfires buried in the sand,
Like the doubloons a pirate might have hidden
Somewhere along the coast, from the beach parties
Where the baby sitter led me on and on;
The bottle rocket we would launch one night

And then forget — until it torched the dune grass,
Unsettling the drifts of sand, the last
Barriers against high tides and tidal waves;
The houses hurricanes yanked out to sea;
The topless women smoking in the sun;
The fear of lockjaw; and the words I hoarded:
Sky, blood, burned, woman, riptide, home, doubloon;
— All driven into memory, into dream.

. . .

The gun emplacements hidden on the bluff,
The bunkers lodged in moss and memory,
In fir and spruce shadow, their lookouts sheathed
In cracked cement and crusts of salt, facing
Northwest, toward the Aleutians and the rumors
Still circulating, like old coins, of war-
Mongering and island-hopping foreigners,

— They're now retreats for lovers. Thus the drained
Madeira bottles, matchbooks, bras and socks.
And the spent rubber sprawling, like a slug,
Next to the rabbits' hutch of broom. And inside
The fort, scratched on the walls: the dank inscriptions
Of those who came before us, the fantasies
And sad graffiti of the spurned, of the dreamers
Who drive us back outside, where we can wash
Ourselves in the light drifting through the trees —

Back to the bearberries and hairy cinquefoil
Clustering on the bluff, and here we catch
Our breath . . .
                    Below us, huddling in the rocks,
A wounded — a nesting gull. There's a cliff swallow
In a dive. A couple marches up the beach.
And the keeper of the lighthouse on the point

Is sleeping (or is it mechanized?). . . Then we're
Unbuttoning each other once again,
Repeating the old words, like a string of waves,
Like whorls chased into shell, panting and poised
On the bluff, between the water and the guns.

. . .

Yet here they are again — gulls scavenging
Through the shells heaped up on the shore and the wrack
Scattered by last night's storm, then taking flight
Over the cove, the memory of the spill
Now just another part of evolution,
Like the reserves of women and old men
Who volunteer to clean the birds and beaches
Whenever tankers founder off the coast.

A long-necked clam reclaiming its spoiled bed
Wriggles out of its collar, like a banker
Returning to his unfaithful wife; while crabs
Float to the foam and surface of the tide pools,
The way certain words rise in a poet's mind
To haunt him — *salt, gold, revelation, war . . .*
And in the ebb tide's froth and lather, rooted
To nothing save the sea: anemones
Bending their blossoms in the wind of the waves.

And here I am, love, scared and on my own
Hands and knees, crushing barnacles to study
These sea-sown flowers, praying the ocean, this blotter,
Will live through our mistakes. And praying, too,
That you and I, having come to the edge
Of the continent and seen how coastlines shift,
How land holds something back before it gives
Way to the pummel of the waves, will learn
In arguments to stifle our desire

To unleash everything we can't abide.

And there you are . . . walking toward the lighthouse
Beyond the distant headland, in rolled-up jeans
And bare feet, in the cold surf, mourning perhaps
The luck we have created for ourselves,
Unmoored and drifting into the separate waters
Of our future — and if not separate, still uncharted,
Like dreams, the nightmare we're yet waking from,
And what will soon belong to memory.

II.

Three Translations

I. Interior

A table set with the grandest luxury
Inordinately long
Divides me from the woman of my life
Woman I see strangely
In the starlight of glasses cut in every shape which keeps her
    tilted backwards
Her neckline plunging in a gust of wind

                        — André Breton

II. Hourly

The sea's measured by waves,
the sky by wings,
ourselves by tears.

Air rests in the leaves,
water in springs,
ourselves in nothing.

And you go out alone,
with us, with no one.

                        — Jaime Sabines

III. Miss X

Miss X, yes, little Miss X
finally showed up, just as I'd hoped:
all eyes —
small, infinite, innocent.
She's limber and clean as the wind,
soft as the dawn,

151

happy and smooth and deep
as grass growing underwater.
Sometimes she's sad
and grieving ghosts, quick
sketches on a mural, cover her face.
I think she's like a child
pestering an old woman,
like a crazy burro entering a city, loaded with hay.
Sometimes a real woman
appears in her eyes, and shakes her by the collar,
and rips out her guts with her tears.
Miss X, yes, the woman who laughs at me,
who won't tell me her name,
puts her hand over her heart, insisting
she loves me but doesn't love me.
I let her waggle her head,
saying no and no — but that gets old.
And when I kiss her hand, seeds
of wings flutter under her skin.

Yesterday the light
was wet all day,
and Miss X went out with her cape
on her shoulders, free and easy.
There's never been such a child, never
such a lover.
Her hair fell over her forehead
into her eyes, into my soul.

Ah, Miss X, Miss X, hidden
flower of the dawn!

And you don't love her, reader, so you don't know.
But I'll be seeing her tomorrow.

— Jaime Sabines

Pike Place Market Variations

Like luck, this cobbled street is short, runs one-way,
And ends abruptly — before you reach the harbor,
Where a young man believes his luck will turn
And the seafarer studying his charts
Will tell you luck, like the weather, is a language
Foreign to the landlocked. Yet since the public
Market this morning is awash in sunlight
Instead of rain, shopkeepers count their blessings,

Like change. One hovers near the register
— A moon drawn by its tides; another dreams
Of moving to Peru; and Sol, the ancient
Fishmonger, oiled and scaled and glistening
In his rubber apron, spins like a new coin
Around Elizabeth, the Flower Lady,
Who clubs him with a bundle of narcissus
And, laughing, soft-shoes toward First Avenue.

The salt wind rises with the tourist trade.
And panhandlers assume their posts, their lookouts.
And the yacht sails fluttering on the Sound
Resemble moths flushed from a sweater drawer.
Down at the waterfront, three travelers
Boarding the ferry bound for the Inland Passage
Trust the drunken captain and his crew
More than the sea, the weather, and their luck.

• • •

The revolutionists in Left Bank Books
Discuss arthritis, another enemy
Sowing its seeds of toxic waste and fire:

What X-rays show, how blood tests work, and why
Joints twist — the burning, the gnarled dance . . . A man
In fatigues cracks his knuckles for his comrades.

A woman with a spike of black-and-white
Hair winces, like the bellows of an accordion.
U2 supplies the music, style, and weather.

Illness is a metaphor, asserts the student
Activist, sticking his pencil in the fan
To stop the blades; while the cash register

Hums on the counter, registering nothing,
Like the clerk locked in his spasm of regret.
In here the customer is always wrong.

That's why the nun and the industrial
Hygienist who met by the Translation shelf
Sidle to the door, exchanging scowls —

And why the classicist appraising poems
For his masseuse would rather be a roofer
Than go on teaching Horace to the young.

And their best seller? A thick manual
On love and war in which the ink is thawing,
Smearing the writer's thesis and his name.

No sign of Celan's ghost, that fugal master
Of silences still floating down the Seine,
His death another *message in a bottle.*

Nor will you find the works of visionaries
Like Rimbaud or Apollinaire. No one
In here speaks French. And the coffee pot is gone.

Outside, on the remaindered table: Che
Posters, *The House of the Dead,* New Directions
Anthologies, French bread, embroidered shorts,

A legal brief, a wadded handkerchief
Containing subway tokens and the spent
Seeds of a soldier from the Russian front . . .

The Chinese merchant from the corner shop
Coaxes a paper snake out of his pocket:
It slithers through a hooker's legs and in

The gutter suns itself; it coils, uncoils;
Strikes at the lamppost; disappears. The hooker
Grins. A cardsharp sniggers, picking his teeth.

An Eskimo on Mad Dog Twenty-Twenty
Wipes froth from his split lip and, reeling after
A Texas banker, blazes a trail to the street.

• • •

Luring the lunch crowd,
The street musician rattles
Against his body's locks
And bars a bent soup spoon.

How he plays the buttons
Pinned to his vest and jeans —
McGovern, Eagleton,
Et cetera — like steel drums.

And tattooes his tattooed arms,
Trading on his skin, like a stripper —
Ankles and elbows, cheeks
And brow. He spins and spins.

Vasectomy! he croons,
Then rings his cracked teeth.
A shoal of hungry people
Drifts toward him. *It only hurts*

For a little while . . . A woman
Tugs her husband's sleeve.
Smiles. A cop nods on his way
To sleep. The people sway.

A blind girl runs her fingers
Through the singer's hair,
The top hat at their feet
Netting grace notes and silver.

. . .

Praise the artisans arranging and rearranging their displays — the
converted bingo tables lining the corridors and colonnade, all the
spaces covered with their handmade wares.

Praise the maker of music boxes, that hoary man tattooed from head
to foot: his indelible snakes, wound round tree trunks and women's
legs, are crinkling, shedding their skins, *his* skin; while from his lit-
tle boxes come the airs and partitas of Bach.

Praise the painter of neon Mt. Rainiers and his chain of canvases
throbbing like gashed thumbs, this bottler of volcanic ash from Mt.
St. Helens in love with Mars, magenta, and the windsock sewer from
Savannah — the woman with the crew cut, whose hanging streamers
twist in flames of silver, cobalt, and crimson, singeing the air.

Praise the young man with the raven perched on his shoulder, the
unemployed actor who gave up waiting tables to learn by heart *The
Collected Poems of Edgar Allan Poe* and then recite them to the

crowd under the awning (though they prefer the troupe of mimes assembling in the street, the men and women dressed in black, whose dumb shows and charades leave tracks in the air — a spoor to follow into the invisible world).

Praise the beekeeper rubbing honey into her ankles and wrists; the man with the green tongue — the realtor-turned-herbalist and spokesman for poultices; the carver of wooden toys and flutes, whose pinwheels will charm a boy even as his squeaky trills drive his customers away; the slender woman singing "Desperadoes" to the runaways in the alley; and Richard Hugo, who found *the primal source of poems: wind, sea and rain, the market and the salmon,* and thus became a source himself.

Praise all the bric-a-brac of scrimshawers, driftwood etchers, collectors of bright shells and curios; and the vegetables gleaming in their baskets — the Walla Walla sweets sprung from their earthen cells, the madder taffetas of romaine lettuce, the corn shucked just enough to tease, the cherries split by rain, the greens and green; and the aroma of Market Spice Tea sweetening the aisles down which busloads of retirees shuffle, their pockets lined with pull tabs lifted from reservations in Arizona and New Mexico; and the salt wind that will blow this all away.

And, remembering the boy in the sleeveless jacket — how he hustles businessmen by the arcade; and the pregnant girl by the fish stand, picking scabs from the tracks on her arms; and the hobo who drags one leg, like a duffel bag, toward the train yard; and the migrant workers in Wenatche — the first to taste our poisoned apples; and the crews of the overloaded crab boats that topple in the Bering Sea and disappear; — remembering them (and others, many others), praise those artists relegated to the open-air stalls, who bask in the sun, then huddle together in the wind and rain, like the bagmen shaping our routes through the Market.

. . .

O savor of salt
             and salmon — the holy
And nomadic chinook
                    neatly filleted in ice;
The king and coho
                  caught by a troller
Or gleaned from a gill net,
                            gulls circling overhead;
And loaves of baked bread
                          steaming in waxed bags,
Salt-rising and sourdough,
                           the settlers' legacy;
And green onions, garlic,
                          goulash, and gazpacho;
And sweet-and-sour pork
                        simmering in the pot
Of the Chinese cook;
                     and chutney; and chocolate;
And lemons and loquats;
                        and loganberry jam;
— All gathered up and garnished
                                in gusts of salt air!

The fishmonger, fattened
                         on fried clams
And beer batter,
                 brandishes his knife
At the cat on the counter.
                          A woman in culottes
Buys ferns and freesias
                        at the flower shop,
Then roams around
                  the crowded block, reading
Menus, a mark
              for the moneyed and the saved.
A futures trader tickles her

                              until she turns away.
A Moonie hails her,
                              and she hurries home
To sear and sauté
                    for someone new.
O nights of white wine
                         and high winds!
O curry, and cayenne,
                               and sweetened cappuccino!

. . .

Here's how the day draws in its nets: schooners,
Purse seiners, customs agents — all converge
On the sea wall protecting Ballard; sieves
In the Pacific tighten their long lines
And strain the water, trapping sea birds and seals
For the connoisseurs of squid; the radar's snares
Widen to catch the clicking of the gears
And meshes in the warships near Malaysia;
And the sun shreds the clouds on the horizon,
Sinking into the future — or the past.

Aboard the listing *Walla Walla,* the ferry
Stalled in the Straits of Juan de Fuca, nervous
Passengers scan the deep for whales, and the crew
Applauds the antics of the gulls and grebes.
The captain has his own agenda: *Skål!*
He mutters to a paper bag and sways
Behind the wheel. In the log book he writes:
Who will salute the sun when I am gone?
Then falls asleep . . . *Untie the captain's shoes,*
The first mate cries, *and make him swim to shore!*

Back at the Market, tattooed with swastikas
And armed with nightsticks, skinheads are goose-stepping

159

In time to music only they can hear,
Taunting the mimes and Eskimos, afraid
Of no one but the truant officer.
A woman with a bomb in her rucksack
Clutches the rainbow-colored sail she lifted
From the sail shop and steers away from them.
Behind the dumpster she will plant her charge,
Setting the homemade timer for tonight.

. . .

Dusk, and a man in a tin space suit selling real
Estate — one-acre lots on the moon: *Drilling rights!*
Certificates! A tax shelter! The Flower Lady
Gives away glads. Sol packs a salmon in dry ice.
Two bagmen look for blankets in the dumpster, wards
Of the weather who will sleep tonight in cardboard quilts.
The artists collect their wares, the cardsharp files his nails,
And the spoonplayer rubs his blackened jaw, his silver.
Streetwalkers, like night-blooming flowers, suddenly
Emerge. A drunken couple waltzes up the block,
Believing their good luck will never change. The sign
Above them — MEET THE PRODUCER — reels in the first stars.

René Char: Three Poems

Here

Here is memory's skimmer
Mist from the miners' pools
Surrounded by smoking linens
Rose star and white rose

O clever caresses, O useless lips!

Love

Being
The first comer.

Lungs

The vision of firearms
The belly's recognition.

Signals

The target? My heart, of course. Heart of magnesium and the stripes of white powder etched into the ground outside the abandoned mill, the tailings which will burn the desert until the sea washes in again. No one understands why the tides keep rising, nor how the shrinking coastlines will affect the shipping lanes. Marriage, too: the charts must be revised — minute by minute.

You, for example: why do I love you like the Roman courtesan who showered on the young Emperor favors known only to the gods and the Minister of Culture? (Culture! I hear you shrieking once again: Handmaiden of the trout stringer left in the stream to foul the water cooling our sacks of wine, wine of the rarest vintages — *Texas Rain, Gold Rush, Shoot the Moon . . .)*

No wind. No matches. And no way out of here tonight. For we have boarded up our bodies and denied the birds their dispensation. Yet we leave our signals everywhere, like spores settling in the ashes of new islands erupting out at sea. Capped by a coral reef, each harbor will remain unnavigable to the innocent — or so the mariner hanging by his thumbs will tell you.

Meantime, a flashlight rips through a cloudburst; and on the outskirts of Los Alamos, where a nighthawk circles an adobe hut and the horse determined to feed on the seedlings just outside the fence is wearing barbed wire like a necklace, Oppenheimer's ghost won't stop taunting the designers of the detonator. As for the operator of the mill? He moved to Phoenix, too.

It's one bright day after another now for those who use their wings to flirt instead of fly. And while certain words have been picked clean of their most odious meanings, the books themselves are usually confined to their stalls, where grooms can wipe the sweat from their backs and blanket them for the night. All the same, jets are dropping from the cloud-burled skies, like leaves.

What will this stamp validate? The moon, which has become the portal of an empty church? The chollas used for crosses? The flash floods lighting up our arroyo? The hailstones and other omens falling from the clear sky? Hail Mary while we're at it — the famous Mary Magdalene, as well as the not-so-famous Mary Ryan, who's waiting, still, for the bus to Toledo.

Elsewhere, the tanker roiled on the reef is spurting oil. Soon the beaches will be tarred and feathered, the gulls sealed in their tombs of clipped wings, the sea itself a flag braided with our greed, waste, and desire. And you, my sad siren, my little wriggler — where are you now? Do you still dream of prying open the day's rusted lid? What scream are you preparing for the ball?

Three Riddles

A moth eating words? A miracle,
I whispered, discovering a worm
Swallowed our speeches whole,
Devoured ideas in the dark.
And that strange thief stole
No wisdom from his meal.

. . .

It hangs like a holster
Under the master's cloak,
Pierced and piercing.
Praise him for using it —
Quickly lifting his garment —
To light the mouth of the cave!

. . .

Covering, uncovering her
Scratched breast, like a poor
Man fingering a diamond
Found in the street — what she felt
In secret, I now feel:
Why else would it sting me?

III.

White Noise

The clocks were going nowhere, like the striking
Plowmen. Snow drifted in the streets; a shroud
Of smoke covered the city; smelters glowed.
And in the mountains, in the pass itself,
Trains stalled along the curves, the engineers
Arguing over the existence of God,
The passengers clamoring for bread and wine,
Afraid of avalanches, like the brakemen
Studying their Bibles and the blank
Expanses above them — ridges and cliffs,

Chutes opened by the wind, the swells ice climbers
Avoided, where high waves of snow had crested.
Near the peaks, weathermen were measuring
Holes in the sky, gathering evidence
For the mayor and his accountants, the straw men
Picketing the plowmen in the valley
And our appointment to the court, we learned,
Would be delayed — for our security,
According to the clerk in the judge's chambers.
A euphemism, we suggested, *for exile?*

No answer. So we stayed an extra night
In that magnificent hotel or palace.
Or were we in a sanitarium?
There were so many herpetologists
Inspecting the aquarium. And doctors
In the spa, debating the merits of a new
Disease. And scores of women in white shifts
Lined up outside the dining room . . . The Gothic
Handwriting on the walls of the library?
Only judicial scholars read it now.

Yet in the morning we were certain nothing

Had changed, although our shoes were missing (no doubt
Stolen by the maid who prowled the halls at dusk,
Crying for the shoeshine boy — the half-wit
Who on his nightly rounds must have been amazed
To find nothing to clean). Outside our door:
Rags. And a stack of oiled and polished shoe trees.
Then the street rigged with another foot of snow,
Plowmen rubbing their hands and legs, and smoke
— Smoke thickening into a gauze of ice.

When the mayor ordered his men to load the cannons
Aimed at the mountains, like a troop of critics
On a deadline, even the vagabonds
Casing the street applauded . . . *But the clocks,*
We shouted to the crowd, *the clocks must be
Our metaphor for all this stammering!*
We pardoned the tongue-tied — the businessmen
Emerging, fevered, from a topless bar,
From groping for the dancers wiping off
Their bodies and the stage. They ignored us.

Into the wild we carried our campaign.
Rags on our feet, we marched up the railroad tracks,
Determined to rouse the hibernating switchmen,
The partisans who had replaced the bears
With gondolas and guardrails. We passed hundreds
Of shovels propped, like crosses, in snowbanks
And irrigation ditches. Passed mule deer
Feeding in a graveyard, pawing the plastic
Flowers which flapped against the tombs and headstones,
Then yanking down the spruces' snow-tipped branches.

Beyond the houses, foothills, and eroding
Benches — the bands and watermarks of a sea
Which had vanished after the Ice Age — we came
To the deserted fort, its walls collapsing

168

Into the barracks. And found statues (crusted
With lichens) of the cannons our ancestors
Had trained on the city, on the towers and steeples
In which heretics once hid, publishing
Articles of confederation and tracts
No one could understand. Nor yet dismiss.

Then crossing streams — the mountain's arteries
Of ice, hardening in the wind. And gasping
For breath in the thin air, sucking on pebbles
To quench our thirst. To soothe our aching feet,
We packed them in snow. Changed our rags. Heard ghosts
Howling. Ghosts of the tribes assimilated
Only into the earth. And trappers still
In their pelts, sharpening their knives and wits,
Soldiers lost to the gold-and-silver rush,
Coolies, like bent spikes, buried by the tracks.

Ghosts of hounds hunted down by wolves. And women
Giving birth by starlight. And rebels burned
On bridges, their ashes spilled into the water
To mix with arsenic leaking from the mines
Upstream . . . And when at last we reached the junction,
When we discovered the switchmen in a shack
Frozen to their controls, we cried out: *Fools!*
Why did you trade the wild for a sinecure?
What will become of our poisoned wells and trees?
Of Rome, and Istanbul, and Walla Walla?

Save us from our extremities! we begged.
The switchmen wouldn't stir. Not for the flags
The brakemen raised, those patriotic sheets
Seized from the laundry and waving like cabooses.
Nor for the smoke signals the passengers
Sent from the dining cars. Nor even the urgent
Messages transmitted between the engineers

And their superiors. Nothing woke them.
They were as lost and peaceful as the clocks
When the cannons started firing at the mountains.

Shells landed near the ridges, and the sleepers
Remained oblivious to the exploding
Snow pack, the drifts sundered from cornices
And cliffs, the way the loosening slabs scraped
The slopes, sliding like pallets off a truck.
The air shook. Windows rattled. And on they slept
Through the roar of wave upon white wave
Cascading down the chutes and swells, breaking
Over the woods, sweeping into the canyon
Stumps, roots, nests, boulders, hunters' cabins, trains

And tracks . . . What could we offer in the way
Of proclamations *now?* Only our numbing
Fingers and feet. Our open mouths. A hush
Settled over the canyon and the steeps,
Like a cold front. No birdsong here nor sign
Of Wren and Raven, Magpie and Hawk. What happened
To the deer? How did the wolves and coyotes fare?
Where did they go? Forgive the switchmen? No.
The mayor and his men? No. And no again
To the engineers drowning in the wet snow.

We shook hands in confusion. Then continued
Marching, retracing the footsteps of the blind
Explorers lost in an icefall, the party
The guides abandoned to the elements.
What did we hope to find? Their maps in Braille?
Perhaps the base camps of deposed dictators
From South America? The Northwest Passage?
The Holy Grail? Nada. We'd given up
Our search for an elixir to hear the spirit
Rappings of wind and water in the mountains.

We had no interest in the missing climbers.
The trains reminded us of businessmen
Bankrupted by a rush on silver. The thieves
Kneeling before a bonfire in the woods,
Garbling their rosaries — only those fallen
Despots who counted their doubloons, like beads,
Might have distracted us. And not for long.
Soon we would tire of listening to them chant
The names of all their enemies, plotting
Against the rain forests, against the poor.

We hurried on, despite our reservations
About the distance to the top. Above
The smoke from the inversion: more storm clouds
Hiding the sky's blue fist. Night with its black
Lung shuffled through the afternoon, wheezing
In the white pines. We knew the maid by now
Had left our shoes with the Salvation Army.
The plowmen were burning their pickets to keep warm.
And the herpetologists? In their seminars
The talk had turned from rodents to the plague.

Past a frozen waterfall, the tracks
Disappeared in a litter of jagged limbs.
On we trudged, panting, waist-deep in the snow,
Until we finally made it to the mines
Abandoned before our birth. Here were the broken
Wagons and wheels. Rust. Ore chutes cinched with bands
Of ice. Slag heaps (which in moonlight would rise
Like bread dusted with flour). We had no feeling
In our feet, but we would never turn back:
Behind us there were only ghosts and smoke.

Up ahead? Ruptured slopes, blood-colored water
Gushing out of the mines, and the vast claims
Of avalanches and icefalls — prospectors,

Weathermen, engineers and arguments,
The climbers who might surface in the spring,
Trailing gloves, boots, ice axes, and the rope
Lashing them together . . . The last miners had nailed
Across the entrance to one shaft a sign:
Bad Air. We looked inside, dropping our watches
In the stream. Took a deep breath. Started climbing.

IV.

Luck

For those not born to wealth or royalty,
Luck's a language learned by fits and starts —

Numbers, dates, an odd word; an alphabet
Of chance from which whole phrases sometimes come,

Then vanish, like water from a desert wash;
An idiom for the inspired, the fevered,

The few; an accent mastered by the young
On trips to Kashmir or Peru, forgotten

On their way home, and in old age perhaps
Rediscovered; — luck's the speech of the streets

Closed to outsiders, sealed off by a look,
A locked gate . . . Rhyme-rich, accentual,

And heavily inflected, it depends
For nuance on a grammar no one's parsed,

On tones beyond the scholar's understanding:
Birdsong, the royal *we*, the signatures

Of heiresses and chief executives,
Who may think luck, like money, speaks everywhere.

. . .

Fixed in its sling of instincts, the hummingbird
Whirls with a whine around a stand of broom

Until it flings itself into the air,
Ricochets off the sky, and disappears,

Striking the fancy of the man who saunters
Along a cliff which overlooks the sea.

He rubs his brow, squinting in the sunlight,
Imagining the end and still believing

Luck's the land Goliath measured off
And lost — the land his conqueror invented,

And with it poetry for a people marked
And mastered by the Word, psalms for their longing . . .

The hummingbird is swinging from the air,
Its courting dance a string tied to the season,

Then knotted by its mate's amused/amazed
Eye. And the man has wandered off the trail,

Past warning signs and guardrails and the tufts
Of beach grass shoring up the bluff, to the cliff

Edge, where he can count the fishing boats
And empty barges returning from Alaska.

Down on the beach: a woman studying
The bleaching bones of trees swept into shore,

A woman who could lead a horse to wine
And make him drink . . . He won't forget her name.

Nor why he came here for the afternoon,
Why he comes here almost every day,

Convinced his luck will change . . . The sea is calm.
The hummer's dance is raveling in a dive

Over the cliff; its mate, it seems, is gone.
Pods open in the broom. Seeds beat their wings.

. . .

Into the wild blue laundry we will go,
A woman opening her window sings —

And throws her husband's dirty clothes to the dogs,
The malamutes that bury bones and belts,

And drag a wooden pallet like a sled,
And guard his fruit trees and his flower beds.

Her blouses billow and unbutton clouds
Of lint collecting in the wicker hamper.

Her children's sheets unfurl in the salt wind,
Sail past the bluff, and head on out to sea.

Her mannequins are drying on the line
— Her foster family . . . *So much depends*

On luck, she has decided, *not rusting tools*
And whitewashed chicken coops . . . And when she dreams,

She dreams about the desert — and the wolf
That lured her father's dogs into the hills,

Where the pack waiting for them on the mesa
Tore them to pieces, leaving only scraps —

Their bones and tags — to sink into the wash . . .
And how in spring the children tunneling

Into arroyos and irrigation ditches

Would learn that skies can crumble without warning —

Yet she escaped into another life,
Where luck's a truer standard than the gold.

It wasn't part of the bloom, sings the woman,
Who could be thinking of the gray wolf's quick

Extinction or the boys who drowned in waves
Of falling dirt, her husband's apple blossoms

Blackening after the surprising snow
Or the way her marriage turned — is turning out.

. . .

The clocks are ticking in the robins' nest —
Blue clocks with hands we cannot read or hold,

Stem-winders whose speckled faces crack, like mirrors,
Revealing luck in one of its disguises:

A flock of chirping robins, hungry as time;
For time begins where luck leaves off — in the nest.

And the nest itself, set in a tree and wound
With twigs and leaves, is ticking in the wind,

Timing another front from Canada,
The clouds and cold air loping over the Sound,

The storm easing into the starting gate —
What isn't timed this early in the spring?

Here's the bird watcher with his hourglass,
The widower who will not leave his perch,

The window where his wife would count each spring
And fall the geese returning to their pond.

Here are the swallows circling the dock and dam,
Spreading their nets of flight to catch mosquitoes

Hatching — on schedule — in the shallow water;
While in the limed grass sweetening the earth

A redbreast scratches up a meal of worms
Sated with Weed & Feed and fungicide,

A diet guaranteed to shape, to mold
And manicure the worms, the birds, the lawn . . .

And here's the shattered mirror in which luck
May change again in seven years, like skin —

Or so the widower has come to think,
Although *his* skin is spotted as the lawn.

The air is turning colder, and the wind
Creases the whitecapped Sound. No Canada

Geese on the pond — and yet he still believes
In resurrection, in the future: the lawn

Will be reseeded . . . What else does he believe?
Luck's the egg containing all his mirrors,

And time's a fledgling learning how to fly,
Then a bird singing by itself at dusk.

. . .

How much depends on luck when empires rise
And fall? On vagaries of will and weather?

Caprices of princesses and conductors? —
The aqueducts are full and falling down.

The markets dip and sway, like belly dancers.
And the sovereign's heading for Byzantium,

Convinced there are reserves of luck, like coal
And diamonds, buried in his vast dominion;

And certain, too (despite the oracle's
Warnings), his absence will not augur change:

How could his ministers exhaust those veins
Providence fills and fills? They won't collapse,

Nor will luck's wellsprings dry up in the heat
Of summer, of the impending celebration

Marking his prosperous and peaceful reign.
Meanwhile, there's a new comet in the sky,

Which for the oracle explains the roads
Unraveling in the countryside and why

The soldiers are retreating from their wives.
What else? Handcarts are washing down the streets.

The barefoot rabble's dribbling a skull
Around the plaza, taunting the condemned,

The hooded men lined up beside the fountain —
Emptied mysteriously late last night.

Bankers and belly dancers join in praising
The way the markets shake off all constraints.

Worse, the court orchestra is out of tune:
Illegible and incomplete, the score

Commissioned for the celebration is
Unplayable, according to the musicians –

Yet the maestro in his miserly
Fashion won't rehearse it anymore.

As for the sovereign and his entourage?
Camped for the night on a high mountain pass,

He worries – once again – about his daughter:
Is she conspiring with her bodyguard?

Marriage or mutiny: what will she do?
And where will he go if she turns on him?

Banish the oracle, he tells his aide.
Banish as well my daughter's new attendant,

Then execute a minister or two –
No sense in taking chances while I'm gone.

. . .

Do accidents obey a set of rules
Invisible to us? Consider X,

Bicycle messenger and activist,
A man who chains himself to railroad tracks,

Who now lies screaming in an intersection,

181

His legs mangled under his mountain bike —

He won't remember why he ran the light
At First and University, ignoring

The ambulance (which, after hitting him,
Can't — or won't — take him to the hospital).

Nor once he is released from Harborview —
Three months hence and wheelchair-bound — will he care.

For now his legs are useless, like his desire
For kinky women and a daily swim;

For shredding tuna nets, and sugaring
Bulldozers' gasoline, and driving spikes

Into trees lumbermen mark for the mill;
For strolling down to the waterfront at dusk . . .

What will remain for him in memory?
How on his lunch break he was reading *Swank,*

And how — stretched out and bleeding in the street,
An angry nurse attending to him — he thought

Of lingerie, of women in lace, in black,
Naked women whose names he'd never learn.

Who are you? he kept crying to the nurse —
And to the life passing before his eyes,

A life bounded by glossy photographs
He neither recognized nor yet dismissed.

And what about his messages, his pouch

Of documents vital to the defense

Of a company accused of dumping arsenic
Into the Sound? Forgotten, lost, or stolen.

And so that case will end in a mistrial —
To the chagrin of the mad witnesses

For the earth's defense . . . Yet if dead fish wash up
Along the beaches and the sand turns blue?

Say the homeowners, organizing, force
The company to change its policies —

He'd praise their efforts if his interest
In activism hadn't disappeared . . .

By then he's thinking accidents, like art,
Have formal patterns, invisible designs.

. . .

In the end our sayings and our saws became
Spells and nets cast over our lives, our debts.

And we repeated all our riddled maxims
Till they formed patterns, which embodied truth

Or charmed the world. (And charmed the sayer, too.)
We said bad luck, like tercets, comes in threes:

One accident begets another, then
Another, then it stops . . . or so we prayed.

We thanked our lucky blues and movie stars.
Threw pinches of salt over the left shoulder

Of Lot's unhappy wife. Avoided cracks
In the binding of our pornographic books . . .

And yet, and yet: the woman cradling
The bruised body of the child thrown from a horse,

The boy dragged by the stirrups up the beach
And left, like wrack, along the water's edge,

Where she would find him twitching in the sun,
Among the opened clam and mussel shells —

What made you curse my family? she cried
First at the sea, then at the sky. It was

A cry heard by a poet silently
Composing on the cliff above the beach,

A man who measured out his syllables
Like a greengrocer counting crates of beans.

And since he couldn't see her, he could dream
Hers was a cry which had no origin

And thus might be translated into verse,
Into his lines falling — to his surprise,

His disappointment — into triplets, a form
(He liked to joke) reserved for obstetricians

And young men laboring in a Romance
Language . . . Yet now his words were spirited

Away from their ancestral homes, and phrases
Rose like Atlantis in his mind: *I am*

A house of strings, he chanted to the wind.
Each room's unraveling like a bad review.

The woman cried and cried until her son
Came to. *What happened to the sea?* he asked.

And where's my horse? Who's riding Miracle?
His mother shook her head in disbelief:

Perhaps the famous Age of Miracles
Consigned to history books was just beginning?

They started home, the woman secretly
Praising the whitecaps gathering offshore,

The way the clouds fissured the sky, luck's chains
And vagaries, even the man on the bluff

Proclaiming something to the sea — the sad
Figure who never saw her . . . What was he watching?

The automated lighthouse flicking on
And off, its beam sinking in the rough water.

The poet wondered why that cry had rhymed
With nothing from his memory: was it

A human cry? Divine? He couldn't say,
Though he believed it might return someday.

Likewise, his faith in the return of seasons;
In all revolving things, like love and verse;

In memory giving way to dream, to art;
In luck — that currency no one can hoard,

Which spends itself and which is like the weather
— Impossible to forecast, or avoid.

The sunlight quivered like a bow, and a storm
Flew toward the coast. On the horizon: fall . . .

Here's what the poet could imagine: stalks
Of kelp lying like alphorns on the beach,

Discarded by the tides locked in the task
Of herding in the waves to graze the shore;

And out at sea a deckhand fastening
A schooner's ropes and sails into position,

Who hears a woman singing at the helm,
Music he might mistake for coordinates,

Orders for navigating through the night . . .
Dusk. The figures on the beach were gone.

The poet knelt, praying to hear that cry,
That song again. And soon it began to rain.

Who knotted all the mirrors, the picture window?
He asked himself before he headed home:

Why was that garden laid out like a noose?
Where does this stairway lead — if not to Rome?

NOTES

"The Mormon Globes": Lines 14-15 refer to the Mormons' invention of an alphabet and language, neither of which took hold among the faithful. *Poisonous meadow* is a translation of a line from Guillaume Apollinaire's "Les Colchiques."

"Cotillions": *En tous cas* is a material used in the construction of clay tennis courts. Made from crushed shells, this surface must be salted daily to retain moisture.

"Scotch Broom: An Inventory": It was Thomas Jefferson who brought Scotch broom from the Old World and planted it in his garden at Monticello, from which it escaped across the country.

"Lupines": "Many of the lupines are poisonous to stock during late summer and early fall . . . As the pods and seeds ripen they produce alkaloids that can be fatal if eaten in sufficient quantities." — John J. Craighead, Frank C. Craighead, Jr., and Ray J. Davis, *A Field Guide to Rocky Mountain Wildflowers*, 1963. Lupines are also called wolfbeans.

"Old Wives' Tales": *Water's my will, and my way* — Theodore Roethke, "Meditation at Oyster River."

"Excerpts from a Commonplace Book": *And Sorrow with her family of Sighs* — Percy Bysshe Shelley, "Adonais."

"The Sirens": *Great Invisibles* — "Man is perhaps not the centre, the *focus* of the universe. One may go so far as to believe that there exist above him, on the animal level, beings whose behaviour is as alien to him as his own must be to the may-fly or the whale." — André Breton, "Prolegomena to a Third Manifesto of Surrealism or Else." *Perfumes of Brazil* — "In one corner was a water-lily pond containing, as did each of the other corners, a large unmade bed. A phonograph blared with German marching songs, while behind a screen fresh coffee roasted continuously, permeating the entire exhibition with 'perfumes of Brazil.'" — Franklin Rosemont, introduction to

What is Surrealism? by André Breton.

"Pike Place Market Variations": *Message in a bottle* — one of Paul Celan's definitions of his poetry. *The primal source of poems: wind, sea and rain, the market and the salmon* — Richard Hugo, "Letter to Kizer from Seattle."

"Three Riddles": The first two riddles are based on Old English riddles; the respective answers are *bookworm* and *key*. The third riddle is a loose translation of two Sanskrit poems.

ABOUT THE AUTHOR

Christopher Merrill's poetry, fiction, essays, and reviews have appeared in many publications, including *The Paris Review, Prairie Schooner, Mississippi Review, Sports Illustrated, Sierra, The Los Angeles Times Book Review,* and *The Pushcart Press: Best of the Small Presses.* He is the author of three collections of poetry — *Workbook, Fevers & Tides,* and *Watch Fire* — and a book of non-fiction, *The Grass of Another Country: A Journey Through the World of Soccer;* his translations include André Breton's *Constellations* and Aleš Debeljak's *Anxious Moments,* which was recently published by White Pine Press. He is also the editor of *Outcroppings: John McPhee in the West, The Forgotten Language: Contemporary Poets and Nature,* and *From the Faraway Nearby: Georgia O'Keeffe as Icon.*

Merrill was selected by W.S. Merwin to receive the 1993 Peter I. B. Lavan Younger Poets Award from the Academy of American Poets. He lives with his violinist wife, Lisa, in Portland, Oregon, where he makes his living as a free-lance journalist.

Writers' Conference
RESERVE BOOK
DATE ON:

RESERVE SUMMER 1999